THE UNTAPPED
POWER
IN PRAISE

Kenneth Hagin Jr.

FAITH LIBRARY
PUBLICATIONS

Unless otherwise indicated, all Scripture quotations in this volume are from the *King James Version* of the Bible.

Fifth Printing 1995

ISBN 0-89276-725-1

In the U.S. write:
Kenneth Hagin Ministries
P.O. Box 50126
Tulsa, OK 74150-0126

In Canada write:
Kenneth Hagin Ministries
P.O. Box 335, Station D,
Etobicoke (Toronto), Ontario
Canada, M9A 4X3

BOOKS BY KENNETH E. HAGIN

* Redeemed From Poverty, Sickness and Spiritual Death
* What Faith Is
* Seven Vital Steps To Receiving the Holy Spirit
* Right and Wrong Thinking
  Prayer Secrets
* Authority of the Believer (foreign only)
* How To Turn Your Faith Loose
  The Key to Scriptural Healing
  Praying To Get Results
  The Present-Day Ministry of Jesus Christ
  The Gift of Prophecy
  Healing Belongs to Us
  The Real Faith
  How You Can Know the Will of God
  Man on Three Dimensions
  The Human Spirit
  Turning Hopeless Situations Around
  Casting Your Cares Upon the Lord
  Seven Steps for Judging Prophecy
* The Interceding Christian
  Faith Food for Autumn
* Faith Food for Winter
  Faith Food for Spring
  Faith Food for Summer
* New Thresholds of Faith
* Prevailing Prayer to Peace
* Concerning Spiritual Gifts
  Bible Faith Study Course
  Bible Prayer Study Course
  The Holy Spirit and His Gifts
* The Ministry Gifts (Study Guide)
  Seven Things You Should Know About Divine Healing
  El Shaddai
  Zoe: The God-Kind of Life
  A Commonsense Guide to Fasting
  Must Christians Suffer?
  The Woman Question
  The Believer's Authority
  Ministering to Your Family
  What To Do When Faith Seems Weak and Victory Lost
  Growing Up, Spiritually
  Bodily Healing and the Atonement (Dr. T.J. McCrossan)
  Exceedingly Growing Faith
  Understanding the Anointing
  I Believe in Visions
  Understanding How To Fight the Good Fight of Faith
  Plans, Purposes, and Pursuits
  How You Can Be Led by the Spirit of God
  A Fresh Anointing
  Classic Sermons
  He Gave Gifts Unto Men:
      A Biblical Perspective of Apostles, Prophets, and Pastors
  The Art of Prayer

Following God's Plan For Your Life
The Triumphant Church: Dominion Over All the Powers of Darkness
Healing Scriptures
Mountain Moving Faith
Love: The Way to Victory
The Price Is Not Greater Than God's Grace (Mrs. Oretha Hagin)

MINIBOOKS (A partial listing)

* * *The New Birth*
* * *Why Tongues?*
* * *In Him*
* * *God's Medicine*
* * *You Can Have What You Say*
* * *Don't Blame God*
* * *Words*
* *Plead Your Case*
* * *How To Keep Your Healing*
* *The Bible Way To Receive the Holy Spirit*
* *I Went to Hell*
* *How To Walk in Love*
* *The Precious Blood of Jesus*
* * *Love Never Fails*
* *How God Taught Me About Prosperity*

BOOKS BY KENNETH HAGIN JR.

* * *Man's Impossibility — God's Possibility*
* *Because of Jesus*
* *How To Make the Dream God Gave You Come True*
* *The Life of Obedience*
* *God's Irresistible Word*
* *Healing: Forever Settled*
* *Don't Quit! Your Faith Will See You Through*
* *The Untapped Power in Praise*
* *Listen to Your Heart*
* *What Comes After Faith?*
* *Speak to Your Mountain!*
* *Come Out of the Valley!*
* *It's Your Move!*
* *God's Victory Plan*

MINIBOOKS (A partial listing)

* * *Faith Worketh by Love*
* * *Seven Hindrances to Healing*
* * *The Past Tense of God's Word*
* *Faith Takes Back What the Devil's Stolen*
* *How To Be a Success in Life*
* *Get Acquainted With God*
* *Unforgiveness*
* *Ministering to the Brokenhearted*

---

*These titles are also available in Spanish. Information about other foreign translations of several of the above titles (i.e., Finnish, French, German, Indonesian, Polish, Russian, etc.) may be obtained by writing to: Kenneth Hagin Ministries, P.O. Box 50126, Tulsa, Oklahoma 74150-0126.

Contents

Chapter 1
The Praise Cure

Many "cures" for the ailments of mankind have been concocted *by* and administered *to* mankind throughout the ages. Cures of various kinds and categories, from old-fashioned home remedies to the most sophisticated modern-day cures, have been lauded as wonder-working remedies to all that ails humanity.

Several years ago, for example, I heard about a "cure" known as "the barefoot cure." The proponents of this cure declared that if people would constantly go barefooted — rain or shine, sleet or snow — it would alleviate every kind of ailment! They believed going barefoot provided a constant cure, and would keep people from contracting any kind of sickness or disease!

I once read an article about another cure known as "the mud-bath cure." In this article, there were pictures of mud baths, which supposedly could even cure depression! To hear some people talk, if you took a mud bath, it would cure you of *anything* that ailed you — from the common cold to cancer!

During the early days of our nation, "medicine" men traveled back and forth across the country peddling bottled "wonder cure-alls" which were supposed to cure practically everything that ailed mankind. Since the world began, people have always tried to concoct so-called "wonder cures" of various forms and fashions that would supposedly miraculously cure mankind of sickness and disease, pain and suffering, and discomfort and distress.

Down through the ages, people have been in search of miraculous cure-alls for their sicknesses and diseases and their aches and pains. People throughout the world today are searching for help and relief from pain and suffering, and many have paid thousands of dollars to find a cure for their ailments. But the Bible tells us about a cure that doesn't cost anything! Someone else paid the price for this cure!

Actually, this cure was the most expensive cure of all to pay for; it cost Jesus Christ, the Son of God, His life. Jesus' death and resurrection provided a cure for you that doesn't cost *you* anything! And if you will administer this cure faithfully, it will work every time. The name of this cure is *the praise cure!*

The greatest cure known to mankind can be found in praising God. The greatest *deliverance* known to man is within the reach of every believer on this earth — and it is found in praising God from a sincere heart of love and gratitude!

In her book, *Healing From Heaven,*¶ Dr. Lilian B. Yeomans tells the story about a woman who went to China as a missionary many years ago when China was open to receiving the gospel. This missionary contracted smallpox. In those days no cure existed for this disease, so doctors could do little for her. If a person contracted smallpox back then, there was no hope — the person just died. It was a deadly disease. This missionary was quarantined in her room, and ugly smallpox marks covered her body from the top of her head to the soles of her feet.

There she was, stricken with a deadly disease with little medical assistance, destitute, and in a faraway country virtually given up to die. She didn't know what to do since there was no cure, so she began to fervently seek the Lord.

The Lord always rewards the diligent seeker, and He always answers sincere, faith-filled prayer, so He spoke to her and told her to *praise* Him for His faithfulness to keep His own Word. Then He showed her a vision of two baskets. One basket contained the test and trial — the smallpox. That basket was full.

The other basket contained her praise, and that basket was only *half* full. The Lord told her the praise basket needed to be filled with praises so it would outweigh the basket of the test and trial. And when the praise basket was full, her healing would be manifested.

As this missionary lay quarantined in her room, she began to fervently praise and worship the Lord day and night. Everyone feared for her life and thought the loud praises coming from her room was little more than the act of a delirious woman. But in spite of all opposition, she continued to praise God.

She sang praises to God from her heart; she did nothing but praise the Lord. She praised Him for His greatness. She praised Him for all that He had ever done for her. She praised Him for His faithfulness to His Word. She praised Him for her healing. She praised God, and praised God, and praised God.

What was the result of such sincere and devoted praise to God? Finally, after several days of heartfelt praise, the Lord showed her that the praise basket was full! She walked out of that quarantined room completely healed! Her skin was as smooth and clear as a child's; no smallpox marks were to be found anywhere on her body.

Before this missionary began her "praise cure," her body had been completely covered with smallpox marks! Can you imagine that! A body covered with smallpox, and yet through heartfelt praise, she walked out of that room totally healed! She had taken *the praise cure*.

Supplication vs. Thanksgiving

A humorous anecdote demonstrating man's lack of true gratitude and praise is told about two angels who supposedly visited the earth every morning. As the story goes, both angels carried baskets, and they would walk throughout the earth. One of the angels had a basket to collect *requests* and the other one had a basket for collecting *thanksgiving*.

In a short time the basket of requests was full and running over. But at the end of the day when these two angels returned to heaven, the angel with the basket of thanksgiving had but a mere two or three weak "thank-yous" in his basket.

Of course that's just a story; although the principle is valid, the story itself has no validity whatsoever in scripture. But I think it illustrates that many times Christians are guilty of being big on requests and a little short on praise.

If only mankind understood the power of God that is released in praise, I believe that would be reversed; we'd be big on praise and we probably wouldn't have to make so many requests!

God's Cure

The praise cure — *God's* cure — is a cure that never fails in any circumstance or situation. And it is both pleasant *and* effective. What's also unusual about this cure is that as you learn how to implement it, this cure will *always* work for you — and there's no charge for it!

The reason this cure is so effective and is guaranteed to bring results is that it is based on God's Word! The praise cure was purchased and put into effect by the blood of the Lord Jesus Christ on Calvary when He paid for our redemption on the Cross.

But even in the Old Testament, God began teaching His children about the praise cure and its benefits. We need to look at some of the mighty exploits the children of Israel experienced as a result of praising God. The Bible says that what the Israelites experienced were examples written for our admonition and benefit (1 Cor. 10:11).

Let's see what God taught the children of Israel about God being able to perform mighty exploits for the Israelites through *the praise cure*.

During the reign of Jehoshaphat the king of Judah, Israel's enemies rose up to destroy their nation. The

6

The Untapped Power in Praise

kings of Moab and Ammon gathered and marshalled their forces together to come against Jehoshaphat and the children of Israel.

2 CHRONICLES 20:1-4
1 It came to pass after this also, that the children of Moab, and the children of Ammon, and with them other beside the Ammonites, came against Jehoshaphat to battle.
2 Then there came some that told Jehoshaphat, saying, There cometh a great multitude against thee from beyond the sea on this side Syria. . . .
3 And Jehoshaphat feared, and set himself to seek the Lord, and proclaimed a fast throughout all Judah.
4 And Judah gathered themselves together, to ask help of the Lord: even out of all the cities of Judah they came to seek the Lord.

When the Moabites and the Ammonites came against the Israelites to try to annihilate them in battle, the Israelites and King Jehoshaphat were greatly afraid. Jehoshaphat proclaimed a fast throughout all of Judah because the Israelites knew they were no match for the enemy. The whole nation of Israel began to pray and seek God for His deliverance.

When all the Israelites were gathered together to seek the Lord, God spoke to them through Jahaziel. In Second Chronicles 20:15-17, we see the Lord giving the Israelites *His* instruction and *His* strategy to defeat the enemy. The Israelites were no match for the enemy without God's help.

2 CHRONICLES 20:14-19
14 Then upon Jahaziel . . . came the Spirit of the

Lord in the midst of the congregation;
15 And he said, Hearken ye, all Judah, and ye
inhabitants of Jerusalem, and thou king Jehosha-
phat, Thus saith the Lord unto you, Be not afraid
nor dismayed by reason of this great multitude;
for THE BATTLE IS NOT YOURS, BUT GOD'S.
16 Tomorrow go ye down against them: behold,
they come up by the cliff of Ziz; and ye shall find
them at the end of the brook, before the wilder-
ness of Jeruel.
17 YE SHALL NOT NEED TO FIGHT IN THIS
BATTLE: set yourselves, stand ye still, and see the
salvation of the Lord with you, O Judah and Jeru-
salem: fear not, nor be dismayed; tomorrow go out
against them: for the Lord will be with you.
18 And Jehoshaphat bowed his head with his face
to the ground: and all Judah and the inhabitants
of Jerusalem fell before the Lord, worshipping the
Lord.
19 And the Levites, of the children of the Koha-
thites, and of the children of the Korhites, stood
up to praise the Lord God of Israel with a loud
voice on high.

The Bible says the Lord is mighty in battle
(Ps. 24:8), so if anyone should know military strategy, it
should be Jesus, the Chief Commander! What did the
Lord tell the Israelites to do?

Did He tell them to call for their mightiest soldiers
and to gather their most powerful weapons? No, He told
them something that made absolutely no sense in the
natural.

The Battle Is the Lord's!

He told them *they* would not need to fight in the battle at all because the battle belonged *to Him*! (If only Christians today would learn that same lesson!)

Then in Second Chronicles 20:16, God even told the Israelites exactly where they would find their enemy: "*. . . behold, they come up by the cliff of Ziz; and ye shall find them at the end of the brook, before the wilderness of Jeruel.*"

But if the Israelites weren't going there to fight the enemy, what were they going there to do? What would be the use of that vast Israelite army going to meet the enemy if they're not supposed to fight?

We have a clue as to what the Israelites were supposed to do in verse 17: The Lord had said through Jahaziel, "*. . . set yourselves, stand ye still. . . .*" In other words, the Lord was instructing the Israelites to simply take their position. What was their position? It was to be one of praise!

How do we know that? Look at what the Lord revealed to Jehoshaphat.

> **2 CHRONICLES 20:20,21**
> **20 And they rose early in the morning, and went forth into the wilderness of Tekoa: and as they went forth, Jehoshaphat stood and said, Hear me, O Judah, and ye inhabitants of Jerusalem; Believe in the Lord your God, so shall ye be established; believe his prophets, so shall ye prosper.**
> **21 And when he had consulted with the people, he appointed SINGERS unto the Lord, and that should PRAISE the beauty of holiness, AS THEY WENT OUT BEFORE THE ARMY, and to say, PRAISE THE LORD; FOR HIS MERCY ENDURETH FOR EVER.**

Evidently in the nighttime the Lord communicated the rest of the battle plan to King Jehoshaphat because when Jehoshaphat arose the next day, he related the plan to the people. They were to go out and meet the enemy with the praises of God in their mouths.

I'm sure Jehoshaphat had been in many battles. As the king of Judah, he was well acquainted with military strategy. For a military commander of his rank and caliber to rally a choir and put them at the head of his mighty fighting men, he must have heard from God! Only God could stage a military strategy like that and successfully pull it off!

After all, in the natural, who ever heard of marching out to do battle against an enemy host with *singers* leading the way, praising God! What military general ever led his mighty fighting men with a choir! But that's exactly what God instructed Jehoshaphat to do. The Israelites were to take a position of praise.

Of course, in the natural, none of this makes sense as sound military strategy. For example, if you've ever been in the military, you know that a reconnaissance team goes out first ahead of the fighting troops to check the lay of the land and to discover the enemy's position.

I served in the United States Army, and in my infantry training we always sent out a reconnaissance team to check out the lay of the land and the enemy's position before the main troops began to move. A reconnaissance team was always sent out before the troops went out.

We were taught in infantry training that it's the

responsibility of a reconnaissance team to spy out the situation and to gather information — *not* to engage in any fighting with the enemy. In fact, if the reconnaissance team does their job properly, the enemy will never know they are in the area.

The reconnaissance team would gather all the information they could about the enemy and report that information to the main forces. Then when the infantry was ready to launch an attack, the infantry knew the exact location of the enemy's gun emplacements, machine gun nests, and mortar hideouts.

The main forces were so well-advised because of the information the reconnaissance team brought back, the infantry could attack the enemy intelligently and effectively.

But the Lord didn't use that kind of military strategy in the battle against the Moabites and Ammonites! Jesus, the Commander in Chief of the Israelite army, knew a better way! The Israelites were to trust *in God* to fight the battle. And the Israelites were to demonstrate their faith and trust in God by praising Him!

Also, the Lord didn't tell the Israelites just to take a *defensive* strategy and merely hold their own against the enemy. The Lord told the Israelites to march out *offensively* against the enemy *but not to fight!*

The Israelites' offensive weapon against the enemy was *praise!* God could have told the Israelites to hold a prayer meeting. Or He could have given them any number of strategies. But instead, He said, "Don't worry about the enemy. *I* will deliver you. Just praise Me and watch Me work"!

Evidently the Lord knew something about conquering the enemy the children of Israel didn't know. Praise is an effective weapon against the enemy! The Lord knew the enemy couldn't tolerate the praises of God's people! Since God *inhabits* the praises of His people (Ps. 22:3), the enemy flees at the sound of praise, because at the sound of heartfelt praise, God comes on the scene!

Jehoshaphat called the Israelite choir together and sent them out ahead of the strong fighting men. Sometimes the plan of God won't always seem to make sense in the natural, as it didn't in this case. But when God gives you the plan and tells you what to do, no matter how foolish it may look to the natural man, it will work every time.

When the Lord tells you to do something, don't lean to your own understanding, just obey Him. First make sure it's Him giving you instructions; if it's God speaking to you, the instructions will line up with the Word of God. Many people try to execute plans in the Name of the Lord that are not from the Lord. What the *Lord* tells you to do always lines up with His Word and it always prospers.

Imagine the reaction of Jehoshaphat's generals when the king put the choir first in the ranks in front of the mighty fighting men, who weren't even allowed to fight! They were supposedly the strong fighting men — the mighty men of valor! Some of those war-torn, rugged veterans had fought many a battle; maybe they thought Jehoshaphat had gone a little too far this time. But *God* had a plan!

Here came the singers leading the way, singing praises to God. An Israelite band may have accompanied them because in the Old Testament the Israelites often made a joyful noise to the Lord with musical instruments. I can imagine the army all arrayed and standing at attention: The javelin throwers, the archers, the mighty men of valor — all lined up in their ranks — with the choir leading the entire army!

I can just see that huge Israelite army as they were standing at attention. The king gave the command to march *and* to sing as they went out to meet the enemy. Maybe an old lieutenant struck up the cadence, "Hup, two, three, four. Hup, two, three, four." About that time maybe they all began to sing, ". . . *Praise the Lord; for his mercy endureth for ever*" (2 Chron. 20:21).

We don't know for sure, but the Israelites may have sung Psalm 136 as they went out to face the enemy because that psalm repeats the refrain, ". . . *for his mercy endureth for ever.*" We *do* know, however, that the Israelites magnified and glorified God with their praise.

Extolling God in the Psalms

Psalm 136 has several sections to it; the first part is a praise to God — the God of gods — and the Great Creator.

PSALM 136:1-9
1   O give thanks unto the Lord; for he is good: for

his mercy endureth for ever.
2   O give thanks unto the God of gods: for his
mercy endureth for ever.
3   O give thanks to the Lord of lords: for his
mercy endureth for ever.
4   To him who alone doeth great wonders: for his
mercy endureth for ever.
5   To him that by wisdom made the heavens: for
his mercy endureth for ever.
6   To him that stretched out the earth above the
waters: for his mercy endureth for ever.
7   To him that made great lights: for his mercy
endureth for ever:
8   The sun to rule by day: for his mercy endureth
for ever:
9   The moon and stars to rule by night: for his
mercy endureth for ever.

This first section of the psalm extols the great God Jehovah. The children of Israel spent considerable time thanking God for who He is — the God of gods and the Lord of lords. They praised Him because He is the great God who set the sun and the moon and the stars into place, and created the vast universe and everything in it.

In the second part of this psalm, the children of Israel praised the God of gods and the Lord of lords for His great delivering power to their forefathers in delivering them from the bondage of Egypt. The Israelites praised God in faith for what He was *going to do* for them, based on what He *had already done* for them, and based on what they knew about His faithfulness.

Christians today need to take a lesson from this! Your faith can be encouraged by looking back at what

God has done for you in the past and the victories He's already won for you.

> **PSALM 136:10-15**
> **10 To him that smote Egypt in their firstborn: for his mercy endureth for ever:**
> **11 And brought out Israel from among them: for his mercy endureth for ever:**
> **12 With a strong hand, and with a stretched out arm: for his mercy endureth for ever.**
> **13 To him which divided the Red sea into parts: for his mercy endureth for ever:**
> **14 And made Israel to pass through the midst of it: for his mercy endureth for ever:**
> **15 But overthrew Pharaoh and his host in the Red sea: for his mercy endureth for ever.**

Can't you just see that Israelite host as they marched toward the enemy singing the refrain, ". . . *for his mercy endureth for ever*"!

As they marched and sang, the miles they had to journey probably just began to fade away behind them as they marched to the cadence of the singing. If you've ever been in the army and done any marching, you know singing takes your mind off how far you've come and how far you've got to go!

When I was in the Army and we used to march, it was easier to sing while you marched because then you didn't think about how heavy that pack on your back was and how tired you were. You just began to focus on the rhythm of the song, and your steps became lighter as they picked up the cadence of the beat. Before you knew it, you'd marched twenty miles.

I imagine the closer the Israelites got to the enemy camp, the more joyful they became because they were so caught up in praising and worshipping the Lord.

In the third part of Psalm 136, the psalmist recounts the victories the Lord had given Israel, and extols God for His greatness.

PSALM 136:16-26
16 To him which led his people through the wilderness: for his mercy endureth for ever.
17 To him which smote great kings: for his mercy endureth for ever:
18 And slew famous kings: for his mercy endureth for ever:
19 Sihon king of the Amorites: for his mercy endureth for ever:
20 And Og the king of Bashan: for his mercy endureth for ever:
21 And gave their land for an heritage: for his mercy endureth for ever:
22 Even an heritage unto Israel his servant: for his mercy endureth for ever:
23 Who remembered us in our low estate: for his mercy endureth for ever:
24 And hath redeemed us from our enemies: for his mercy endureth for ever.
25 Who giveth food to all flesh: for his mercy endureth for ever.
26 O give thanks unto the God of heaven: for his mercy endureth for ever.

The third part of Psalm 136 exalts the Lord for bringing the children of Israel into the land of Canaan, their Promised Land. They praised Him for all the great victories He had given them in their lives. They praised Him because He had delivered the enemy into their hand.

Many principles for Christians today regarding praise lie hidden in Psalm 136. We are to praise and worship God for who He is, and we are to praise Him for what He's done for us in the past. Recounting your past victories in Christ will encourage you that God is going to help you in your present circumstances.

When depression tries to get ahold of you, and you begin to experience trials and you're tempted to become discouraged, stop and reflect on *who God is*. Reflect on the God of the universe who created the earth and the stars and the planets. Concentrate on the greatness of God, and try to imagine how big He really is. Then praise and thank Him because He's big enough to meet your need!

Recount Your Victories

Then rehearse what God has done for you in the past. Look at all the past victories He's given to you, and give Him praise and honor and glory for them. When you rehearse your victories in God, you'll be ready to praise and thank Him for the victories He's winning for you right now — even though you may only see those victories with the eye of faith.

As the Israelites marched and sang, they may have rehearsed their past victories in God, singing about how the Lord had overthrown great kings for them and delivered nations into their hands in times past.

And as the Israelites marched and praised God —
going out to win a battle they would never fight — and
as they recounted their victories in God — their faith in
God grew strong!

That's exactly what will happen to us if we will
praise God when we encounter difficulties — our faith
will grow strong! We don't need to fight our own battles!
We can depend upon the Lord to fight our battles for us!

I can just imagine the Israelite singers boldly pro-
claiming, "God has redeemed us from our enemies, for
His mercy endures forever. We're fearless against any
foe because our God fights for us! The battle is not
ours — it's God's!"

The Lord's Military Strategy

Let's see how effective the Lord's military strategy
of praise proved to be!

2 CHRONICLES 20:22-25
**22 And WHEN they began to SING and to PRAISE,
THE LORD SET AMBUSHMENTS against the children of Ammon, Moab, and mount Seir, which
were come against Judah; and THEY WERE SMIT-
TEN.**
**23 For the children of Ammon and Moab stood up
against the inhabitants of mount Seir, utterly to
slay and destroy them: and when they had made
an end of the inhabitants of Seir, EVERY ONE
HELPED TO DESTROY ANOTHER.**
**24 And when Judah came toward the watch tower
in the wilderness, they looked unto the multitude,
and, behold, they were dead bodies fallen to the**

earth, and NONE ESCAPED.
**25 And when Jehoshaphat and his people came to
take away the spoil of them, they found among
them in abundance both riches with the dead bodies, and precious jewels, which they stripped off
for themselves, more than they could carry away:
and they were three days in gathering of the spoil,
it was so much.**

As those singers led the Israelite army, praising the
Lord and worshipping Him in the beauty of holiness,
the Bible says their enemies turned against each other
and destroyed themselves!

Just the day before, the Israelites were trembling
because of the enemy, but because they obeyed the Lord
and got in line with *His* plan, their enemy was thor-
oughly defeated. In fact, there was so much plunder
and spoils of war that it took three days for the
Israelites to collect all the valuables!

We don't know how God caused the enemy to fight
one another. It's just speculation, but maybe God
caused the enemy to hear the Israelites singing about
the great God of deliverance and of His mighty con-
quests in battle. Maybe that threw the enemy into such
panic they turned on one another in confusion.

Or maybe God took an immense "heavenly" micro-
phone and amplified the sound of the Israelite singers
with enormous "supernatural" speakers, so when the
enemy heard the noise, it sounded like a great host of
people. Maybe the enemy said, "We don't have a
chance!" and began to argue and fight amongst themselves until they killed one another off.

We do know that when the Israelites approached the enemy camp, not one enemy soldier was alive. The fighting was all over! The Lord had done exactly what He said He would do. The Lord fought the battle for the Israelites. The children of Israel didn't even have to draw their swords! The battle was the Lord's, and the victory was the Lord's! Now that's good strategy!

What can Christians today learn from this account? For one thing, God is always on His children's side. It doesn't matter whether it was the children of Israel living under the Old Covenant, or whether it's His born-again children living under the New Covenant today, God always helps His children! He always comes to our rescue.

The enemy of God, Satan, is in the world today (2 Cor 4:4). He tries to come against the Church of the Lord Jesus Christ to utterly destroy it. But the Bible says that no weapon formed against us shall prosper (Isa. 54:17). The battle is not ours — we do not need to fight our own battles in life. God says He will fight our battles for us!

Satan Is Defeated

Besides, the Lord has already defeated Satan at the Cross. So if we would quit magnifying Satan and giving him so much credit and just focus instead on the wonder-working God who fights our battles for us, we would see with our own eyes the victories we long for!

If the devil has been trying to bombard you with

temptations, tests, and trials, remember, the battle is
not yours, it's God's! You don't have to try to "fight"
Satan. Just stand your ground with the Word of God
and then begin to praise God that He is performing for
you what He has promised you in His Word (Rom. 4:21;
Heb. 10:23).

There will be circumstances in life that will look
impossible *to you*. But if you are to stand firm and
immovable on God's Word, believing Him to fight every
battle for you, you will need to learn the power in
praise.

Learn to give God praise and glory in the midst of
every trying circumstance — *before* those obstacles
and circumstances change! Give God praise and glory
for what He has promised you in His Word — even
though you don't see any change in your circumstances
because that's faith! And faith always wins the victory
(1 John 5:4)!

If you know who you are in Christ, and the devil
starts coming against you, you can throw your shoulders back and begin to march like a true soldier of God
with the helmet of salvation intact, and your shield of
faith raised high. You can boldly proclaim the promises
of God, singing and praising God confidently for the victory, and you shall prevail!

Church, it's time the Lord's army begins to *march*
forward and *praise* God! It's time we use the praises of
God to come against the crises the devil tries to throw
at us!

Praise God in Spite of Circumstances

We need to learn to give praise and glory to God in the face of every obstacle *before we see the victory*. If we'll learn how to praise God, we'll see victory every time, no matter how bleak the circumstances may look.

I'm not saying we are to praise God *for* the trial or *for* the sickness or *for* the test Satan may be trying to bring against us. I don't believe the Bible says we are to praise God *because* we don't have money to pay our bills or *because* we can't feed our families.

You don't praise God *for* the evil circumstances; you praise God *in spite of* the circumstances. The focus isn't to be on praising God for the sickness or disease or the test or trial; the focus is on praising God no matter what may occur because your trust is in Him to see you through to victory.

You are to praise God *in faith* because He's already delivered you. Faith is praising God *before* you see God's delivering power actually demonstrated in your behalf. That's exactly what the children of Israel did, and that's why they were successful.

But when the children of Israel went out to face the enemy, they just *praised God*; they didn't ask for anything. You see, when your life is on the line, you'll make sure you're doing exactly what God told you to do, and you'll make sure you do it with your whole heart! And God had told the Israelites their victory was in praise!

Many Christians today think praising God consists only of mouthing, "Praise God," "Praise God," a few times. Then almost immediately they're demanding again, "Lord, gimme, gimme, gimme"! But that's not the kind of praise that moves God!

A Way Out of Depression

The next time depression tries to come upon you or circumstances begin to pile up round about you and try to overwhelm you, don't bow down and accept defeat! The best way to get rid of depression is to sing praises to God. You don't have to keep asking God to deliver you. The Bible says the promises of God are yea and amen (2 Cor 1:20). So just begin to praise the Lord when circumstances try to overwhelm you. Depression and the enemy's oppression can't stay in your life when your heart is full of praise.

Sometimes in dire circumstances you hear people say, "Let's call a fast! We need to pray all night so God will hear us!" No, you don't. Just call a "praise meeting," even if you're just by yourself, and begin to whole-heartedly praise the Lord.

If God could rout the enemy in the Old Testament with the praises of the children of Israel — people who were not born again — think what He can do with the praises of His born-again children! Learn the lesson of praise! Look at this battle the Israelites won by praise, and take a lesson from it.

Learn to sing God's praises when the enemy tries to come against you. Certainly, you should take authority over the enemy in the Name of Jesus, but then focus all

your attention on the Lord by praising Him. As you do
this, the devil will have to flee from you.

I believe there is a "cure" we can receive from God
through praising and worshipping Him. In fact, I
believe we can attain to the highest level of faith and
victory as we learn how to continually praise and worship God as a lifestyle, regardless of our circumstances
because praise keeps our attention focused on God.

Take Your Position of Praise

If the devil has been trying to bombard you with
temptations, tests, and trials, do what God told the
Israelites to do! Take your position of praise! God is saying the same thing to you that He said to Israel in
Second Chronicles 20:15-17: "Don't be afraid! The battle
is not yours, it's Mine! Stand on My Word and praise
Me. I'll take care of you, if you will trust Me!"

Realize trials can be overcome and victories can be
gained through praising and worshipping God. You can
receive healing by praising and worshipping God,
because praise and worship is the language of faith.
And God's Word says healing has already been provided
for us (Isa. 53:5; 1 Peter 2:24; Matt. 8:17). You can
receive from God whatever the Word promises you by
simply acting in faith on the Word by praising and
thanking God.

In today's world, it seems that many Christians are
talking about the devil and magnifying what he's doing
more than they are magnifying God and what *He* is

doing! They magnify and exalt the devil by constantly telling what the devil is doing in their lives! I don't care what the devil is doing; he has already been defeated by Jesus Christ. I want to know what God is doing on the earth today.

Other Christians are so devil-conscious and fearful of the enemy that they're always trying to tiptoe past the devil, so to speak. And if they ever do praise the Lord, they whisper because they're afraid the devil will hear it! But he's just the one who should hear God's people praising the Lord! We need to tap into the power that is released in praising the Lord!

The Christian's "Canaan Land" is taking possession in this life of what is already rightfully ours in Christ. Taking possession of our inheritance in Christ is much the same spiritually as taking Canaan land was in the natural for the children of Israel.

In other words, natural giants opposed the children of Israel; spiritual "giants" try to oppose us. However, those "giants" have already been defeated in Jesus' triumph over them at the Cross (Col. 2:15).

Canaan land is not a type of heaven because there are no battles or giants to fight, no cities to take or kings to overthrow in heaven. Canaan land is a type of the Christian's life down here on earth. In this life there are battles to win and giants to overcome. But there's no power of the enemy that can stand against you when you learn how to stand on God's Word and praise God!

Go forth with the praises of God in your mouth! Don't look at the "giant" that may be standing in your way — the test or trial that tries to threaten you to keep you from possessing the promises of God for your life. Look only to God and to His Word. Give Him praise because what He has promised you, He is also able to perform (Rom. 4:21).

---

[1] Lilian B. Yeomans, M.D., *Healing From Heaven* (1926, Springfield, Missouri: Gospel Publishing House, 1973), pp. 57, 58.

Chapter 2
Your Spiritual Jerichos

Jericho was the first battle the Israelites fought after they crossed the Jordan to go in and take possession of their Promised Land. God again gave the Israelites the plan for taking this city and winning this battle *without a fight*! This battle, too, was to be won with the high praises of God in their mouths and with a shout of victory!

> **JOSHUA 6:1-5**
> **1 Now Jericho was straitly shut up because of the children of Israel: none went out, and none came in.**
> **2 And the Lord said unto Joshua, See, I have given into thine hand Jericho, and the king thereof, and the mighty men of valour.**
> **3 And ye shall compass the city, all ye men of war, and go round about the city once. Thus shalt thou do six days.**
> **4 And seven priests shall bear before the ark seven trumpets of rams' horns: and the seventh day ye shall compass the city seven times, and the priests shall blow with the trumpets.**
> **5 And it shall come to pass, that when they make a long blast with the ram's horn, and when ye hear the sound of the trumpet, all the people shall shout with a great shout; and the wall of the city shall fall down flat, and the people shall ascend up every man straight before him.**

Jericho, the first city the children of Israel took for their possession as they journeyed toward Canaan, was not won by fighting a battle! Think about that! God

instructed the Israelites to march around Jericho every
day without making a sound. They had their marching
orders even though in the natural the instructions
didn't seem to make any sense. Then on the seventh
day, the Israelites were to march around Jericho seven
times.

The seventh time as they blew the trumpet and
shouted and praised God, the walls fell down. The
Israelites simply went in and took possession of *what
God had promised them*! The Israelites didn't fight in
this battle; they just obeyed God's instructions, shouting and praising God, and God gave them the victory.

Yes, in order for Christians living under the New
Covenant to possess our "Canaan land," we, too, will
have our spiritual Jerichos we must take for God's
glory. God has placed desires and goals in each one of
our hearts — pursuits and dreams that are *His* will for
our lives. We all have our Jerichos we need to possess.
But *God* has promised to give us our spiritual Jerichos!
It will be done by *His* power and for *His* glory, not by
our own might or strength, and we will give *Him* all the
praise for it!

Our Christian experience on earth is in a spiritual
sense what going through life was in the natural for the
children of Israel. The Israelites fought natural enemies that loomed as giants. Our warfare is not against
natural enemies, but against supernatural enemies
that sometimes seem to loom as giants. However, under
the New Covenant, our enemy, Satan, has already been
defeated by the Lord Jesus Christ! We need only to

stand our ground in Jesus' victory, declaring God's Word, and praising God for our triumph in Christ.

God didn't promise that you wouldn't have some spiritual Jerichos that you would encounter in life. But He did promise that through *Him* you can conquer every spiritual Jericho because He promised you the victory in *every* circumstance in life through Christ (1 Cor. 15:57; 2 Cor. 2:14).

Therefore, when you come up against your spiritual Jerichos, begin to encompass them one by one with the Word of God: "Greater is He who is in me than he who is in the world!" "I can do all things through Christ who strengthens me." "By His stripes I am healed." "I am *more* than a conqueror through Christ." "God always promises me the victory in every circumstance!" "All of my needs are met according to God's riches in glory through Christ Jesus" (1 John 4:4; Phil. 4:13; 1 Peter 2:24; Rom. 8:37; 2 Cor. 2:14; Phil. 4:19).

After you've stood your ground with the Word, then demonstrate your faith in God's miracle-working power to give you your rightful possession *by praising Him.* As you praise God wholeheartedly in faith, watch those walls or obstacles as they fall down in front of you! No devil, nor any evil circumstance can stay in your presence when you learn how to praise God sincerely with your whole heart!

Many Christians need God to put some spiritual backbone in them because when they come up against a spiritual battle about the size of a mole hill and they stub their toe on it, immediately they're defeated! Then they cry to God, "Oh, God! Why did you let this to happen to me!"

God doesn't bring adversity into the lives of His children; He's not the one who causes those things to happen to you (John 10:10; James 1:17). The Bible says Satan is your adversary (1 Peter 5:8). God didn't say you wouldn't have any tests or trials in life, but He did promise to give you the victory in Christ in every test and trial.

But you have to do as the Israelites were instructed: *". . . Believe in the Lord your God, so shall ye be established . . ."* (2 Chron. 20:20). You're going to have to believe God's Word before you can be established and prosper in this life! And you demonstrate what you believe by praising God in absolute confidence in His Word!

> **JOSHUA 6:16,20**
> **16 And it came to pass at the seventh time, when the priests blew with the trumpets, Joshua said unto the people, Shout; for the Lord hath given you the city. . . .**
> **20 So the people shouted when the priests blew with the trumpets: and it came to pass, when the people heard the sound of the trumpet, and the people shouted with a great shout, that the wall fell down flat, so that the people went up into the city, every man straight before him, and they took the city.**

When the Israelites encompassed Jericho, they blew trumpets and the people shouted with a loud voice. I don't think those Israelites just gave a simple Texas yell either! I think they shouted praises to the Jehovah God. No barrier could withstand *that power* because the Israelites were following *God's* plan. When they shouted unto God, those walls came down and gave way to the power of God!

Do you want the walls that have tried to hinder you to fall down right in front of you, so you can march in and take what God has promised you? Begin to shout and praise God with a voice of triumph because you know who you are in Christ. Shout and praise God with a voice of triumph because you are fully persuaded that what God has promised, He is able also to perform!

Every time in life you come up against a spiritual Jericho, don't let it make you afraid. You have the victory in Christ! Simply begin to march around those impossibilities with shouts of victory, praising God in advance for your triumph.

Faith *believes*. Faith *trusts*. Therefore, faith *praises*! Boldly proclaim your faith in God even though a "Jericho" may be standing right in your way! Don't let that frighten you! That's no obstacle to God! Demonstrate your confidence in God by praising Him even before that Jericho falls down in front of you, and then stand back and watch *God* work. Obstacles can't stay in the presence of God's people when they sincerely praise the Lord for His greatness and His faithfulness to His Word.

You see, when we learn how to truly praise God in absolute trust and confidence in His Word, we won't have some of the problems we've had in the past believing God and receiving from Him. Why is that? Because *praising God strengthens our faith.* The Bible says, for example, that Abraham ". . . grew strong and was empowered by faith as he gave praise and glory to God" (Rom. 4:20 *Amp.*).

And we also saw in Second Chronicles chapter 20 that praise was used as an *offensive* weapon of battle against the enemy, not just a *defensive* weapon of protection. The Israelites won a major battle through the offensive weapon of praise and worship.

If God could use the praises of the children of Israel to defeat the enemy, and they were just natural people — they weren't born again by the blood of Jesus — how much more can God use our praise, the praise of born-again sons and daughters to overcome and defeat the devil's schemes!

Of course the devil is going to try to throw up barriers and roadblocks to our faith in this life. He doesn't want us to receive what God has promised us, so the devil is going to try to build impossible obstacles and put impenetrable barriers across our paths. But we've got to learn how to stand against him, even when it seems as if we're surrounded on every side by insurmountable obstacles.

Those Insurmountable Barriers

When I was in the Army, our platoon drill sergeant seemed to delight in putting us through long, grueling marching drills. Our company was the last regiment to train using the old M 1 rifle. Since this was the last time anyone was going to use that particular rifle before it would become obsolete, the general decided to have a great marching contest commemorating the event. A platoon from every company of the training regiment was chosen to participate in this contest.

On graduation day, all the platoons from each company were to march in competition to win the trophy for the best marching team. They had to march on the parade ground in view of the general who would decide which platoon was the champion. Our colonel had already informed us that our company had better win the trophy — or else! He wanted that trophy permanently displayed in his office!

When we began our marching training for the first time as raw recruits, and the drill sergeant called out, "Attention!" for the first time, we all stood there at attention, scared to death. The first time we began to march, we were so clumsy and inept, we practically ran over one another coming and going. We didn't know how to march! We were raw recruits. We'd been in the army exactly one week and two days.

After the announcement was made about the marching contest, our drill sergeant declared, "*This* platoon is going to win the trophy for the colonel on graduation day! Every evening after chow when everyone else has free time, this platoon is going out on the parade field to march until after dark until you learn how to march like real soldiers!"

So we marched and we marched and we marched.

Every evening after everyone else was finished for the day, we were out on that field marching, "Hup, two, three, four," back and forth, back and forth. We marched until it got dark, and then we marched by the light of the moon! The first time we marched, we were a pretty clumsy-looking outfit; we kept running over one another because we didn't know the first thing about marching.

Marching those many hours, we'd sing when we got tired, because it kept our minds off how tired we really were. After about five weeks of this endless marching, our drill sergeant said, "Take the sheaths off your bayonets, and put them in your ammunition belt."

When you're marching with a bunch of raw recruits with unsheathed bayonets, you'd better watch out! The first time the sergeant calls out, "To the rear, march!" you'd better hope everyone turns the same direction at the same time or else you'd better duck in a hurry! Otherwise, someone is going to get hurt!

When the drill sergeant gave the command, "To the rear, march!" men were turning every which way. You could hear metal striking metal as bayonets clicked overhead. I was never so glad in all my life that I was in the front row!

I looked behind me and one ole recruit remarked, "Now I know why we wear these steel pots on our heads! If it hadn't been for this helmet, I'd be in a mess right now!" Someone had slashed him on the side of his helmet with his bayonet as he had attempted to obey that command!

Finally, after four or five weeks of marching every evening, the drill sergeant brought the company commander out to watch us march. By that time we'd gotten pretty good. When you've marched as many hours as we marched, you finally learn; good marching form just becomes a part of you.

As the drill sergeant and company commander watched us march, the drill sergeant who had been so tough on us had to admit, "I believe you can win that trophy! You're one of the best platoons I've worked with. I'm just going to march you around and show you off a little!" He marched us by another company that was practicing, and they looked terrible! They looked like we had when we first started marching.

Many times in training the drill sergeant would march us down a certain stretch of asphalt road. At the very end of that road was a big ten-foot-high block wall. The drill sergeant would usually march us down the road to the wall, and about ten or fifteen feet before we got to the wall, he'd give the command, "To the rear, march!" and we'd turn around and march back. But this time he wanted to see what we were made of. He marched us down that asphalt road and he never gave us the marching command to turn around.

As we steadily approached that block wall, I could see there wasn't any way to go over it or around it. In fact, there wasn't anyplace else *to* go at all but to run smack into that wall! But the drill sergeant never paused in his cadence, "Hup, two, three, four," as we got closer and closer and closer to that barrier.

We kept on marching, "Hup, two, three, four." I stole a glance at the man next to me, and as he looked at me, the drill sergeant yelled, "Eyes front!" We snapped our eyes to the front in a hurry!

I was on the front row with all the other squad leaders, who all happened to be from Texas too. Finally, that wall was right in front of us. The sergeant never gave us a "To the rear, march" command, so we just marched right up to the wall.

As the four of us on the front row stood in front of that wall — our noses pressed right up against it — every time the sergeant said, "Hup!" our left knees came up and struck the wall. Every time he gave the two or four count, our right knees came up and hit the wall. But we just kept marching, pressed hard against that wall. I determined to obey that command until the wall gave way and we could march right over the top of it, or the sergeant gave us the command, "To the rear, march!"

As it turned out, after that test of obedience, every one of us on the front row wore holes in our fatigues and had to buy new ones! But we had our marching orders so we didn't flinch. I don't know how long we marched pressed up against that wall, but it seemed like a *long* time.

You see, we'd been trained that we were to keep marching no matter what the obstacle was. No matter what came across our path — truck, car, animal, or *whatever* — we had our marching orders. We were not to stop marching for any reason, unless we were given the command to do so. With our noses pressed hard against that wall, we couldn't see anything else *but* that wall. You talk about an insurmountable obstacle! But we had been given our marching orders. However, in the end, that kind of discipline paid off because we won the marching contest!

Many times we Christians go through similar experiences spiritually. The enemy places seemingly insurmountable barriers in our way as we march down the road of life. But we've got our marching orders from Jesus, so we can't break our stride! And sometimes when we march up against the walls of adversity, we are required of the Lord just to stand there and march. In other words, we are required to just stand our ground using God's Word! That's obedience!

There are times in life when it will take that kind of determination to overcome the devil in the circumstances of life. You will just have to stand there and march obediently even when you're up against overwhelming odds. You'll have to take your stand against Satan with the Word of God, not looking to the right or to the left, and most of all, never once breaking your stride in faith!

Marching Orders From the Lord!

In my Christian walk, Satan has thrown up some seemingly insurmountable obstacles in front of me as I've been marching along my road in life. But although Satan has put up walls right in front of my face, I just kept on marching because I had my marching orders from the Lord.

When you have your marching orders from the Lord and you see a barrier in your way, don't stop to look around for a way out. Don't try to dig under that obstacle, crawl over it, or go around it. Just keep on marching, standing on the promises of God as you march. Don't even break your stride or the cadence of your step in obedience to what the Lord told you to do. Just keep marching, but with all your might diligently quote the Word in the face of every barrier or obstacle.

"All of my needs are met according to God's riches in glory." "Greater is He who is in me than he who is in the world." "I cannot fail with the Greater One on the inside." And keep on marching.

Your situation may seem to get darker and darker, as you feel that you're marching right into the night. But if you'll keep on marching and praising God, sooner than you may think, you'll hear a crack in that barrier and daylight will dawn for you.

If you're diligent to stand on God's Word in faith and give Him the praise due His Name for His faithfulness to His promises, sooner than you think that barrier will begin to fall away from you so you can march over the top of it — the victor! Begin to praise God for His wonderful faithfulness to His promises.

Praise God, because His mercy endures forever! Nothing can stop a child of God when he learns how to praise God from the depths of his heart!

In the Army when we were up against literal barriers such as that block wall, many times we found that it helped to sing. We could forget the fact that our bodies were tired and aching if we could sing and get our minds off the wearisome circumstances.

In your Christian life, when you feel like you've got your nose against the wall but you're marching in obedience to the Heavenly Commander, begin to sing praises to God as you march.

Singing the high praises of God will lift your spirit and help bring those circumstances into perspective. Singing God's praises helps you focus on Him and makes those circumstances diminish in size compared to the greatness of God. Your help comes from God, so look to Him, not at what you're going through. Sing God's praises and lift your eyes up to focus on the God who is more than enough and who is big enough to rescue you!

There may be times you will be tempted to doubt what God has promised you. But if you will just stand fast in obedience to the promises of God when the howling storms of doubt and fear try to assail you, and praise God in the midst of every test or trial, God will arise and show Himself strong in your behalf. He is faithful who promised (Heb. 10:23).

And when the enemy puts up barriers in front of you, knock them down with the Word of God! One of God's promises to you is that you are more than a conqueror in Christ (Rom. 8:37)!

You will find that if you will march according to God's "marching orders," and stand on the promises of

God, all of a sudden that wall — that adversity that's come against you — will begin to crumble and crack. Yes, you may have to put your nose right up against that wall, and stand your ground determinedly with the Word of God, but eventually that barrier *must* give way to you. That's because God promises that if you're walking in line with God's Word in every area of your life, no weapon that is formed against you can prosper (Isa. 54:17).

As you stand on the Word and praise God, that barrier — no matter what it is — must come down! But, remember, the more you magnify your problem by talking and complaining about it, the bigger that problem — the wall — becomes! But the Word of God promises there is nothing that can stand against the power of God! God promises that you can march over any barrier by the power of the Lord Jesus Christ, giving God all the praise and glory!

We are to march right over those barriers of the enemy and overcome his schemes and shout the victory! In this army you and I are in, we are promised the victory by our Commander in Chief, the Lord Jesus Christ, no matter what the skirmish, battle, or confrontation! Watch your mountains fall away when you begin to stand on God's Word and praise the Lord for *His* victory and deliverance in your life!

Certainly the circumstances of life will test you. You'll have an opportunity to see what you're made of. After all, it's easy to praise God when everything is going good — when the sun is shining and the breeze is gently blowing and you can smell the sweet aroma of the flowers! But what are you going to do when you are standing on the deck of life's ship and the sun is obscured by dark storm clouds and the thrashing waves rise high and menacingly above you on the sea of life?

What are you going to do then — when the crises of life seem to be rolling in like the waves of the sea tossed in a storm? When you don't have enough money to pay your bills! The kids are sick. The car is broken down. The plumbing won't work. Everything seems to be going wrong! That's when it really counts *what* you do! But I'll tell you one thing, *there is no remedy in griping and complaining.*

You may say, "What's going on? I've been believing God! Why is the devil attacking me! I didn't think there would be any problems when I'm believing God! I thought if I walked by faith, everything would automatically go smoothly. I didn't think I would have any more problems!"

That's not what the Bible says. The Bible says that the trial of your faith is more precious than gold (1 Peter 1:7). It also says, *"Knowing this, that the trying of your faith worketh patience"* (James 1:3). The Bible also says you will have the victory in Christ if you will stand your ground with the Word and steadfastly believe God (2 Cor. 2:14; Isa. 55:11).

When circumstances look the worst — when the circumstances are the *bleakest* and the *blackest* — that's not the time to get weak in faith! That's the time to boldly proclaim God's praises for His faithfulness to His

Word! I know what I'm talking about; I've been there.

The Storms of Life

The crises of life come to us all. I know what it's like to stand against the enemy armed with nothing but the Word of God and the praises of God in my mouth! I've been there!

Several years ago, the enemy came into my camp and tried to destroy my wife and me and our son, Craig! On January 25, 1983, at 2:15 in the afternoon, four doctors looked me straight in the eye and the announcement was made, "Your son has a brain tumor! Unless we remove that tumor, he will die."

I know what it's like when every circumstance looks bleak! And particularly when someone tells you something like that, you don't feel like praising God! You're too numb to feel like doing anything! Words are inadequate to describe how you feel in a situation like that.

After the doctors gave me that dreadful report, I asked them to let me have some time alone. I began to pray. If you've been diligent to hide God's Word in your heart and you know how to yield to the Holy Spirit, in desperate moments like these, the Greater One on the inside will take over. He will rise up big on the inside of you and be your Comforter!

Thank the Lord, I had laid a foundation in my heart with the Word of God. I knew what the Word of God said. If you don't put God's Word in your heart, when the crises of life come — and they come to us all — you won't have anything to lean on or stand on.

In that bleak situation in the midst of utter despair, I lifted my hands and began to praise God. I began to declare, "Greater is He who is in me, than he that is in the world! The devil will not destroy us. He will not destroy my son! With God on our side, we cannot be defeated. God is with us and He is for us. And if God is for us, *who can be against us*!"

Yes, I know what it is to walk through the valley of the shadow of death. It's a fiery trial! I know what it's like to have my nose pressed hard against an insurmountable barrier with the devil all the while screaming at me at the top of his voice, "You've preached God's miracle-working power, but now God is *not* going to come through for *you*!"

I know what it's like to see nothing but despair on every side. I know what it is to watch my son go into an operating room, knowing all the time that my only hope is in God. I know what it's like to have all my faith centered in God because in the natural the situation is hopeless! Yes, doctors have skill, but God alone does miracles!

My wife and I waited 12 hours in that hospital waiting room — from 7 o'clock in the morning to 7 o'clock at night! We praised God all day long! Finally, the doctor, who is also a man of God, came out of the operating room, and I could see the strain he had been under written on his face. He said, "Thank God, everything is fine! Let's give glory to God!" and we praised and glorified God some more!

And that was one of those circumstances in life when after the initial victory, we had to continue to praise God and continue to stand in faith. The doctor informed us that the skull bone would never grow back where they had drilled through into Craig's brain, because Craig was too old for new bone to grow. They also said the ridge of the tumor was still left in the brain; they couldn't remove that part of it without endangering Craig's life.

You can't give up when circumstances don't go your way. That's not the time to give up; that's the time to dig deeper into God! My wife and I determined before God that we would not be satisfied with second best. So we kept praising God and believing Him for every trace of that tumor to disappear and for new bone to grow where the doctor had said it was impossible.

God had assured us that our son would come through this and that his recovery would be perfect. So we continued to praise God for a perfect recovery, and a normal and healthy teenaged son. I praised God in the nighttime, and I praised Him everywhere I went! I continually praised God.

And when the devil would come against me with fear and doubt, sometimes I would get off by myself and just pray and sing praises to God. No, I don't have a singing voice, but God didn't care. He could hear my heart! I would sing at the top of my voice, "Praise God, for His mercy endures for ever! Praise God! I will not be satisfied with second best. Father, we're going to have Your best in Craig's healing!"

The devil is a liar! When my son was released from the hospital, he weighed 90 pounds even though he was 13 years old. But within 6 months, he weighed 125 pounds, and when he was a freshman in high school, he decided he wanted to play *football* of all things!

We had been standing in faith for his complete healing, but before he could play football, we had to take him back to the doctor for an examination.

When we took him back to the doctor for a CAT scan, that ridge of the tumor was completely gone! Not only that but the doctor also announced, "I told you that the bone in his skull would never grow back, but it has grown back," and he showed us the X ray.

Nothing Is Impossible With God

We had received our miracle from God! New bone had grown where that hole had been. The doctor had said that was medically impossible! But nothing is impossible with God (Luke 1:37)! Craig gained 45 pounds after that and went on to play high school football!

Today our son Craig is perfectly healthy and normal. I believe the reason for his miraculous recovery was that we continued to stand our ground and to praise God even when everything looked the bleakest. We came out on top because God's Word promises us the impossible in every adverse circumstance!

God is no respecter of persons (Acts 10:34). The Lord is rich in mercy to all who call upon His Name

(Rom. 10:12). If God can perform the impossible in our lives through His mercy and grace, He can perform the impossible in your life too!

Dare to stand upon God's Word for your miracle! Dare to thank and praise God for your miracle before you see it manifested in the natural! There's power in the Name of Jesus and in singing His praises!

Whatever you are facing in your life, if you will learn how to praise God before you see your answer, God will give you victory! Whatever you need from God, it's available right now if you'll just begin to take God at His Word and praise Him for the provisions He's already made for you in His Word!

You don't need to have someone help you praise God. You don't have to call the prayer line, or get your pastor to help you. You can just begin to call on God and praise Him for yourself, and watch your *impossible* situation become *possible* with God!

Yes, you might have to stand in an attitude of praise for a period of time. Your situation may not change overnight; your victory may not fall on you like ripe cherries falling off of a tree.

But if you're faithful to put your trust in God and in His Word and praise Him for the outcome, the day will come when you will see your victory with your own eyes! Refuse to give up! Stay in God's Presence, and you will see your faith gloriously rewarded!

The praises of God demolish the walls of adversity the devil has meant for harm. Praise causes those walls and barriers to crumble and fall. When they fall down in front of you, then you can walk free in the light and liberty of God's Word! Those walls the enemy has raised to threaten and tower over you must crumble and fall, because when you're standing your ground in faith in God's Word, no weapon formed against you can prosper!

When those enemy walls tumble and fall, you will sing and shout and rejoice with joy unspeakable. Jesus has already purchased your victory for you, so stand your ground with the Word of God! Your victory is assured if you will continue to praise God confidently standing on His Word. Praise Him for His greatness and mercy, and you will see your victory come to pass.

God cannot lie! He has stated it in His Word (Num. 23:19). What He has promised you, He is able to perform (Rom. 4:21)! He has promised He would give you victory in every circumstance in Christ Jesus (2 Cor. 2:14). And even in the Old Testament, God gave us many examples of His people triumphing over the enemy when they trusted in and praised God. Just obey God and sing His praises!

Praises Bubbling Up

One day as I began to pray and praise God, I had a most refreshing experience. I shut myself away where no one else could hear me, and I began to praise God with a loud voice. I probably sang and praised God for about an hour and a half.

All of a sudden as I was singing and praising God, from deep within me the praises of God just began to bubble up and roll out of me in a supernatural dimension. It was like a river of supernatural praise springing up from within me through the power of the Holy Spirit.

Sometimes you can just begin to praise God yourself in the natural, and then the Spirit of God will take hold with you, and you will find supernatural praises coming up from deep within your spirit! I extolled and praised God by a supernatural unction of the Holy Spirit. As I was caught up in praising Him, the Lord began to reveal answers to situations that I had been praying about for a long time.

Think of that! Answers to perplexing problems came as I was praising God! The praise cure is the greatest cure that has ever been known to mankind. God instituted it a long time ago and it has never failed. Nothing stirs the heart of God more than sincere, heartfelt praise. The praises of God's people ascend unto Him as a sweet-smelling aroma.

It does not matter what you need from God — the Word of God has declared that God has blessed us with all spiritual blessings in Christ Jesus (Eph. 1:3). God has your answer for you! But you'll have to learn how to appropriate by faith what already belongs to you. And one way you do that is by sincere, heartfelt praise, because praise says, "Thank You, Father. By faith I have my answer now!"

You can have anything you need from God if you'll learn to constantly praise God and walk in the light of His Word.

Praise God in the midst of despair, when all is dark round about you and you don't see your answer anywhere. Even when the circumstances of life look gloomy, stand your ground and begin to praise the Lord.

In fact, when it's darkest all around you, and the storm clouds of adversity have come rolling in, that's the time to use one of your greatest offensive weapons against the enemy — the high praises of God in your mouth!

Sin, sickness, and disease are our adversaries; they are the tools of the enemy (John 10:10; Acts 10:38; 1 John 3:8). When the devil is blowing his howling winds of doubt and unbelief and trying to get you to walk by sight instead of by faith, that's the time to declare, "I don't care what I *see*! I don't care what I *feel*! I have the promises of God's Word on my side! My God is more than able to meet my needs. My God will see me through!"

And if you'll keep praising God, and keep trusting Him in the midst of adversity, God will make sure that no weapon formed against you will prosper. Satan tries to form the weapon of sickness and disease against God's people. Satan is telling some Christians they are going to be stricken with cancer or heart disease! He is telling others they will fail in life, and their God-given dreams will never come true.

That's why praise is so vital to the Christian. Because praise allows you to rise above your circumstances and those doubts and fears, and causes you to come up higher and get a fresh perspective of your circumstances through God's viewpoint. If you will stand on God's Word and begin to confess His Word over your situation, praising Him all the while, no matter how hopeless it looks, God will completely turn your situation around!

As you praise God — even as you gaze into that darkness that threatens to surround you, God will cause you to come up higher where you can see a golden glimmer of hope on the horizon. Keep your eyes fixed on God as you praise Him and stand upon His Word! And that hope will grow brighter and brighter, until soon you will be on the other side of that mountain that Satan once declared was immovable!

Look up! For your redemption draws nigh. That's the power of God that's unleashed in praise on your behalf through your faith in Jesus Christ. As you keep praising God, you will see the power of God begin to dispel the darkness and untangle the circumstances until you're walking free in the bright sunshine of the liberty of God.

Then you'll look around for your problems, and you won't be able to find them. *Then* you'll look around for the gloom the enemy tried to bind you up with, and you won't find it. The high praises of God from your lips releases the power of God in your behalf to dispel the enemy's schemes.

Adverse circumstances can't hinder or hamper the power of God from being manifest on your behalf! No weapon can prosper against *God's* power. Satan will try to tell you that *your* problems are unsolvable. But God can set you free from *anything* the enemy has tried to use against you. You activate God's power by faith in His Word and the high praises of God in your mouth. Walk in obedience to God's Word, praise Him, and watch *God* unravel your problems! Our God is a problem solver!

God's people cannot be defeated if they will only keep their eyes on Him and learn to stand upon His Word in absolute confidence and trust, praising Him all the while even when circumstances look the worst. I learned a long time ago that if you won't quit, with God on your side, nothing in life can defeat you. God has promised us the victory in every circumstance through Christ. That's *His* promise! And He is faithful who has promised (Rom. 4:21; Heb. 10:23; Heb. 11:11).

I don't believe in quitting! The devil may try his tactics and his maneuvers, but if you just won't quit, and with the praises of God in your heart and mouth, you cannot be defeated.

The power of God is real! The power of God is always available to set you free, but you tap into it by praise. You bring the demonstration of God's power into *your circumstances* by praising Him! If you'll learn how to praise God, the power of God will come on the scene to set you free!

It's easy to jump and shout and praise God when your Christian friends around you are praising God — when the atmosphere is charged with the anointing and power of God. It's easy to sing the praises of God when the congregation is praising God too. But it's another thing to praise God in the bleakest of circumstances, when all you have are the promises of God's Word to stand upon.

But if you'll learn to praise God in those times of greatest need, that's when God makes you *strong in faith*! Then there's nothing that can defeat you, for you've learned the secret of praise. No devil or evil circumstance can overcome you! No power of the enemy can overtake you! You're the *victor* in Christ, not the *victim*!

The power of God is activated through praise because praise is the language of faith. If you will learn how to praise God, you can be set free from any problem, test, or trial. Get ready to receive when you begin to praise God!

If you've been facing a series of tests and trials in your life, and you feel like you just can't take any more, begin to praise God with your whole heart. As I've said many times, when the supernatural comes into contact with the natural, it makes an explosive force for God!

It's true! The power of God is tangible; many times you can *feel* it. God's power is like electricity. You can't see electricity, but if you get ahold of it, you sure can feel it!

That's the way the power of God is. You can't always see it, but when it touches your life and changes your circumstances, you know it!

God wants the Body of Christ to experience the power in praise. When you're facing a problem or when you're facing a need, tap into the power of God that's available through praise. You may not feel like praising God. Usually when everything looks bleak, that's the last thing you *feel* like doing.

But if you will learn to praise God regardless of your circumstances, the power of God will come on the scene. As you spend time in His Presence praising Him, you'll find that your cares, worries, frustrations, and fears disappear in the light of God's Word and His power.

Chapter 3
Praise: A Way of Life!

My heart is fixed, O God, my heart is fixed: I will sing and give praise.

— Psalm 57:7

God, the Creator of heaven and earth, is pleased with our praises. How can we praise God enough for all He has done for us and for all He *is doing* for us? Many times if we only understood that God was working on our behalf behind the scenes, so to speak, we'd be praising Him night and day! That's why it's important *to learn to live in the praises of God.*

When you open your eyes in the morning, instead of perhaps groaning and grumbling, "Oh, no, another day," practice *praising* God. When that alarm clock goes off in the morning, train yourself to say, "Praise the Lord! This is the day the Lord has made. I *will* rejoice and be glad in it!"

The Benefits of Praise

Watch your attitudes change as you practice praising God early in the morning! In some instances, you will probably have to change your thinking. For example, instead of waking up thinking negative thoughts, you may have to consciously *practice* praising God. But if you will do this consistently, you will find your attitudes changing from the negative to the positive.

In fact, you will find that praising God affects your entire day. You talk about the *benefits* of God! When you begin your day with the praises of God on your lips, watch the benefits of God increase in your life because you are tapping into a hidden reservoir of God's power!

As you grow in this remarkable experience of beginning your day praising God and living a lifestyle of praise, instead of feeling irritable and disagreeable, you will discover a new strength and vitality in your life.

Even your family will notice the difference in you! When everyone else is still trying to wake up in the morning, you'll be smiling and singing and praising God! Praising God first thing in the morning gives you an entirely different outlook on your day because *praising God encourages your heart.*

Praise is such an important element in the Christian life because of what it does for *us.* But I sometimes think Christians have relegated this wonderful avenue of receiving God's power and blessing in their lives just to Sunday morning worship services.

Praise is to hold a far greater place than that in our lives! For one thing, the Bible says the joy of the Lord is the Christian's strength (Neh. 8:10), and praise is what ushers us into that joy. The joy of the Lord is always available to us, but praise allows us to tap into that source of strength!

Praise is extolling God for what He has done for us: *"I will remember the works of the Lord: surely I will remember thy wonders of old"* (Ps. 77:11). And praise can be quiet and soft spoken or it can be loud and expressive.

Wherever you are, you can praise the Lord, and it will bring encouragement to your spirit and be a continual source of strength to your life. And praise can change the very spiritual atmosphere of a home! Wherever the praises of God abound, a tremendously uplifting and enthusiastic atmosphere also prevails.

Whether you realize it or not, praising God greatly affects our emotions too. Even though we are spiritual beings, we also have an emotional nature. Man's nature, both on a spiritual level and on an emotion level, is affected by praising the Lord. And we can help keep our emotions in line with the Word of God and stabilized by the praises that come forth out of our hearts — from our innermost being.

I'm sure we've all experienced what a negative attitude and a negative confession does to our lives. The more you talk about how bad you feel and how depressed you are, the worse your condition becomes. On the other hand, the more you begin to praise God for what He is doing for you, the better you feel and the brighter your life will begin to look.

Praising God replaces hopelessness with hope. Praising God for His goodness dispels doubt, gloom, and unbelief. Praise is so important to the believer because it provides an avenue to help you stay in faith and to rise above the negative emotions that would try to bring you down into the arena of doubt and unbelief. And when you're in faith, nothing is impossible to you *with God* (Luke 1:37).

You may not feel you have everything you desire in life. You may even look around at others who seem to have so much more than you do. But to succeed in God, you're going to have to stay on the positive side in your thinking.

So when you start feeling sorry for yourself, instead of just centering on yourself, look around you and find someone to bless who is less fortunate than you are. You will always be better off than many people, so practice looking at your life positively rather than negatively. When you do, you will learn the secret of praising God regardless of your outward circumstances, and you will realize the treasure of a grateful and giving heart.

This principle of gratitude to God for the blessings we enjoy was made especially real to me one day as I talked with some RHEMA students who had come from a foreign country. When they first came to America from Dominica and saw all the abundance we enjoy here, they realized they couldn't afford to get used to living the typical abundant American lifestyle. So they purposely allotted only $32 a month for food while they lived in the United States.

They intentionally allotted this small amount of money for food in order to maintain the same lifestyle they were accustomed to in Dominica. They explained that by maintaining their previous living standards, the privation of their own country wouldn't be such an adjustment for them when they returned to their own villages.

You see, they were from a third-world country, and they knew they had to return to their country. They didn't want to make it unnecessarily hard on themselves to return to Africa, so they wouldn't allow themselves to get used to too much American "luxury." In their country, an *average* American lifestyle is considered *luxury*!

When I visited Kenya, one of the national pastors told me of his difficulties in sending young native men to Bible school in Europe and the United States. These native Africans became so accustomed to the abundance of the city life, they didn't want to return to the bush and minister to their own people! Or if they finally did return to Africa, they only wanted to live in the modern urban cities where they could enjoy the same comforts they had in the big cities abroad!

No matter what country we live in, instead of feeling sorry for ourselves because of unfavorable or unpleasant circumstances, we need to begin to praise God for the blessings He has bestowed on us.

Selfishness Hinders the Blessings of God

I believe one reason many Christians aren't enjoying more of the blessings of God than they are is that they are selfish with what God *does* give them! They believe God for prosperity, and when God begins to prosper them, instead of sharing their abundance with needy people, they just squander the blessings of God on themselves.

And many times a lack of gratitude accompanies this attitude of selfishness. Selfish Christians continue to heap more pleasures upon themselves, and they never think about the needs of others. God can't ultimately bless a person like that with His best.

One of the benefits of praise is that it takes your eyes off of yourself and puts them on God. Praise helps you overcome a selfish attitude because as you spend time in the Presence of your Heavenly Father, He begins to change you and work on those areas of selfishness or ingratitude.

Praise Brings Victory

A defeated Christian is one who does not understand the hidden benefits and blessings in praising the Lord. I have never seen a defeated Christian who lived a life of praise before God. On the other hand, I have never seen a victorious Christian who wasn't continually praising the Lord! Victorious Christians seem to have a positive outlook on life and a grateful attitude in their hearts toward God; they delight in praising their Heavenly Father.

When you're enthusiastic and excited about God, it's a natural expression of your gratitude to praise and thank God for His blessings. You can't be victorious without being grateful to God and praising Him for what He's done for you.

People may express their praise to God differently. Some people are naturally more boisterous and expressive than others because their personalities are just more expressive and outgoing; therefore, they may be louder and more demonstrative in their praise than other people. But we shouldn't criticize anyone for not praising God the way we think they should. What *is* important is to praise God with one's whole heart. The Bible says, *"I will praise thee with my whole heart . . ."* (Ps. 138:1).

However, it might be a benefit for those Christians who are more quiet in spirit to get off by themselves from time to time and praise God wholeheartedly with a loud voice. Sometimes it might do them good just to shut all the doors or get in their car and drive down the highway by themselves, and lift their voice in praise to their Heavenly Father.

Some people would probably scare themselves if they ever heard the sound of their *own* voice praising God out loud! It may sound strange, but some people have difficulty preaching because they're afraid of the sound of their own voice! Actually, when we're praising God in church, we should forget about who might hear us, and just pour our hearts out to God. Then watch the power of God move in our services!

A Joyful Church Is a Victorious Church

A church that doesn't express joyful praise is many times a defeated church. Stop and think about that for a moment! A church with a defeated spirit has no joyful praise. In some churches, you never hear people raise their voices to praise and worship God. Everyone sings practically at a whisper, and no one dares pray out loud. And if anyone were to raise his voice to praise God, the ushers would probably escort him out in a hurry!

Churches like that seem to demonstrate the attitude, *What irreverence! Imagine praising God in church!* But I know as a pastor, it's encouraging for me to see people show their love for God by praising Him.

Basically our praise services should reflect our deep reverence for God. Our praise and worship should reflect hearts and lives of people who are excited about their Heavenly Father. After all, when we go to sports events, some of us get excited and jump up and down and shout about our favorite team.

If we can get excited about a football player running for a touchdown, we should be able to not only deeply reverence but also to be thrilled about Jesus Christ who redeemed us! It's time we learned to value and esteem what's really worthy of our praise — and that's the Lord Jesus Christ and our Heavenly Father!

Our singing in church should also reflect our praise of God. Much of our singing in church is enjoyable, but it's not really *praise.* Genuine praise must flow from the *heart* of man to God. Next time you're praising God in church, ask yourself this question: *Am I just going through the motions of praising God? Or am I praising God from the depths of my heart?*

There's a vast difference between routinely singing praise songs, and singing them from the depths of your heart out of an attitude of gratitude to God. Sometimes words of praise can come out of your mouth, but your heart really isn't involved at all. And that's not genuine praise.

One indication of such "mechanical" praise is a blank, expressionless face because you're just mouthing words. You can even keep time to the music with your hands and do the Charismatic "hop-shuffle." But all that is not *necessarily* true praise! On the other hand, if your heart is involved, it *is* true praise.

But most of the time when we praise God mechanically like that and our hearts are not involved, our minds are a million miles away too. And sometimes people can be so concerned about staying on the beat, they couldn't possibly be praising God because they're too busy keeping time to the music!

In other words, just because people wave their arms and go through the motions of praising God, it is no sign they are *really* praising God. Many people do that when really their hearts are far from God. When that is the case, praise becomes more of a physical exercise than anything else. When these people get finished, they've had fifteen minutes of aerobic exercise — not praise!

I don't think Christians do this intentionally. But when we praise God mechanically, instead of it being an *inward* heart expression, praise becomes little more than an *outward* mechanical act or display. There's a vast difference between true praise and worship that comes from our *hearts*, and the mechanical expressions that just come from our *lips*. True praise comes from man's spirit or heart and is expressed through his lips.

Another mark of true praise is that when we sing in church, for example, we don't "perform"; we praise God from our hearts. The songs themselves should reflect our praise and worship of God. In other words, the music shouldn't draw our attention and focus *away* from God to man or anything else; it should draw our attention and focus *to* God and His magnificence and power.

Praise music needs to reflect our deepest sentiments of praise and worship to God, not just be nice words with a catchy beat. But sometimes, particularly in some of the more modern upbeat choruses, the beat and the rhythm of the songs can have a tendency to draw our attention to the music rather than to God. And some music just appeals to our *emotions*, not to our *spirits*. Music that appeals to our carnal natures or souls can actually hinder us from worshipping God.

In fact, some praise songs are strictly soulish; they appeal to the emotions of man, not to his spirit. But when our music expresses praise to God for His greatness and honors Him for what He has done for us in our redemption, that kind of music goes beyond a mere superficial, soulish excitement. True praise penetrates deeply in the realm of the spirit and pleases God. True praise also edifies and builds up one's own *spirit*.

Music Is a Powerful Praise Tool

We need to be particularly careful in the area of

church music for two reasons. One reason we need to be careful has to do with the origin of music. When you study the Bible, you find that Lucifer was originally in charge of music. Lucifer was God's chief musician (Ezek. 28:13,14). When Lucifer rebelled against God and fell, Lucifer perverted the purpose of music so music would be used to worship him, not God.

Another reason we need to be careful about our church music is that almost nothing has the ability to affect the human nature and emotions of man more than music. Music is to have a positive, not a negative effect on us. Music can help lead believers into praise and worship, or it can hinder them from worshipping God.

Musical instruments were originally created to praise God. The Bible has much to say about musical instruments being used to praise the Lord, but the devil has tried to pervert music and use musical instruments to praise *him*, not God.

However, that shouldn't prevent Christians from using musical instruments as God originally intended — to praise the Lord! Many people seem to think we shouldn't have beautiful music in church; they seem to think church should be as sober and sedate as a funeral parlor! But we should use music to praise and glorify God!

The church needs to return to true biblical praise and worship in music. In true praise and worship, the congregation is drawn into a state of reverence, praise, and worship to God in their *spirits*. True praise and worship is not a physical or a soulish experience.

In the beginning of the Charismatic Movement, Charismatics criticized denominational churches for their rituals and mechanical liturgical services. And Charismatics criticized Pentecostals for their excessive repetitive singing.

But have we Charismatics fallen into our own kind of rituals and pitfalls? In some instances, I think we may have. For example, we've grown accustomed to singing certain songs in a certain way and we consider that worship. But do we Charismatics now have our *own kind* of rituals?

Let's just make sure our praise in church is genuine and not something that's worked up, performed, or put on mechanically. In other words, let's avoid praise that's just an outward fleshly demonstration, and let's praise God with our whole hearts.

True Praise Glorifies God — *Not* Man

PSALM 50:23
23 Whoso offereth praise GLORIFIETH ME. . . .

True praise is precious in the sight of the Lord. True praise glorifies *God* and takes our eyes off *man*. True praise and worship exalts God alone and gets our eyes off man and personalities.

The Body of Christ needs to learn the difference between true praise and worship, and an outward fleshly demonstration of praise and worship. Some

Charismatics have taken what my father, Rev. Kenneth E. Hagin, taught on New Testament praise and worship out of the context in which it was meant.

For example, there's a time and place for everything, and clapping is appropriate in certain instances and at certain times — but *not* in the middle of the pastor's sermon! Clapping is *not* appropriate when someone is giving a prophecy or speaking a message in tongues and interpretation, or when the Holy Spirit is moving in any of the other manifestations of the Spirit.

For instance, if the Holy Spirit is moving in the manifestation of the gifts of healings, that's not the time to start clapping. When the Holy Spirit is moving in power and demonstration, that is the time for a congregation to maintain an attitude of reverence for what God is doing so that the Spirit of God is not hindered by fleshly displays from accomplishing what He wants to do.

A congregation can dissipate the moving of the Holy Spirit if they are not taught to reverence God when He's moving by His Spirit. There is a time and a place for all things. Expressions of rejoicing and joyful outbursts of thanksgiving for what God is doing is appropriate during the praise service.

Clapping your hands in church when you're keeping time to the rhythm of the music is fine, so long as you realize *that* is not praise or worship; that's just keeping time to the music. And in certain instances such as this, particularly for certain kinds of music, it may be appropriate to clap your hands.

We can express our joyful thanksgiving to God with expressions of shouts and joy. But we must realize there are deeper moves of the Spirit of God when such demonstrations would not be appropriate. Deeper moves of the Spirit of God require and merit deeper reverence.

During deeper moves of the Spirit of God, fleshly demonstrations grieve the Spirit of God and hinder Him from moving as He desires. And I'm convinced from a biblical standpoint that upraised hands and man's heart and mouth filled with praise are more pleasing to God than man's mere *applause*.

Therefore, as a deeper more biblical expression of praise and worship, why not lift our hands to God as a demonstration of complete and total surrender to Jesus Christ, the King of kings and the Lord of lords? When our hearts *and* our mouths are filled with praise and worship, and our only desire is to bless God's holy Name, such praise is well-pleasing to our Heavenly Father.

Do you see the difference? I believe if the Body of Christ could realize the difference between the superficial, mechanical praise that is little more than an outward fleshly demonstration, and the genuine praise and worship that flows from the heart as a demonstration of the Spirit and of power, God could move the Body of Christ into an area of the demonstration of the Spirit we have not yet experienced.

Of course, we must realize that the devil wants believers to remain in a superficial, fleshly and soulish state of praise rather than to come into a deeper level of

Spirit-led, Spirit-motivated praise and worship. If the enemy can keep us in an emotional, superficial state of praise, he can hinder us from receiving benefits God the Father desires us to have.

We will not be able to receive some of the benefits of God as long as we remain in carnal, fleshly realms. Until we move into the deeper praise and worship that comes from man's heart, God is hindered from releasing His power to the Body of Christ in greater measures. Jesus said man was to worship God in Spirit and in truth (John 4:23,24).

And again, the test of true praise and worship is that it draws you closer to God, not to the flesh, and not to man. For example, in church when people sing praises to God, we can close our eyes and forget about the singers and just listen to the words of the song and worship God.

Music that is *designed* to glorify God draws us closer to God. The Spirit of God can come upon musicians and they can play a spiritual song under the direction and inspiration of the Spirit which the entire congregation can enjoy.

When it's done by the inspiration of the Spirit of God, music such as this will draw the congregation into worship. This is anointed praise and worship by the inspiration of the Holy Spirit. When musicians are playing upon musical instruments, we can forget about the musicians and just let the godly music draw us closer to God in worship.

I believe the more we come in line with New Testament principles and practices of praise and worship, the deeper the move of the Spirit of God will be in our church services.

Praise is extolling God for what He has *done* and *is doing* for you. Worship is extolling God simply for *who He is*. There is a difference. Many Christians have not learned to distinguish the difference between praise and worship. Therefore, shifting from praise to worship and back to praise again in a service can sometimes hinder people from being able to reach a place of true worship.

For example, if congregations begin praising God in a robust style which is normally more conducive for praise, but then immediately try to worship God, they may be hindered from entering into worship. Once they do reach a pinnacle of worship, if the pace is once again quickened to a faster style more conducive for praise — it may be difficult for a spirit of reverence in worship to flow. In other words, flip-flopping back and forth and in and out from praise to worship and back again can hinder a congregation from attaining a real pinnacle in worship.

It will help a congregation attain a height in their praise and worship services if they will follow the leading and guidance of the Holy Spirit and some simple considerations.

For example, it is helpful to assist a congregation attain a height in the praise and worship service if they will continue in an attitude of praise for a time, and *then* move into worship. Or they can continue in praise if that's the way the Spirit of God seems to be leading. Or many times a congregation can move directly into worship, and then they should continue in worship.

A definite orderly progression is helpful to maximize our praise and worship services to the glory of God. If congregations will learn how to move and flow with the Spirit of God in an orderly fashion, God will be able to perfect our praise and worship in the local assembly and manifest Himself to a greater degree.

Reach Out in Faith

Many times in the local body when the congregation is praising and worshipping God, the Holy Spirit moves in such a way that if you need healing or anything else from the Lord, you can just reach out in faith and appropriate what you need for yourself. In an atmosphere of true praise and worship, by simple faith and praise you can appropriate the healing that already belongs to you in redemption.

Many Christians today have been healed by the power of God just sitting in the congregation listening to the Word of God being preached. They would be dead today if it hadn't been for God's healing touch. Those who have been delivered from death's door, so to speak, by the power of God have something to praise God about! They praise God with a whole heart!

We can take a lesson from people with a dynamic praise life. Some of us need to learn to express our praise with our whole hearts. Much depends upon our attitude of heart. Are we praising God with a loud voice to be seen of man so we can look pious? Or are we really praising God from our hearts because we love Him and because we believe His promises?

You see, praise allows you to be able to tap into the healing virtue of the Lord Jesus Christ. Jesus is always willing to heal you, but praise is a wonderful demonstration of your faith, enabling you to praise God for the answer before you actually see it manifested! Also, many times when you have pain in your body, and you begin to praise God in simple faith for your healing, every symptom of pain will leave.

True praise stimulates and invigorates faith, enabling you to thank God in faith for your answer before you see it manifested. In other words, true praise and worship in a church service creates an atmosphere and prepares hearts to receive from God.

Praise refreshes you physically too. Many times when you're tired and you praise the Lord, your body will begin to feel strengthened and invigorated.

God Gives Sleep to His Beloved

What are some of the other benefits of praising God? One benefit of praise is a very practical one. Some Christians have chronic sleeping disorders and it is with great difficulty they are finally able to get to sleep at night. Many times if they would just begin to praise God, they would be able to fall asleep. Then the next thing they would be aware of is waking up in the morning!

Praising God quiets your natural carnal mind. Praise also quiets the body and allows you to enter into God's peace and rest so you can drift easily off to sleep. Learn to "praise" yourself to sleep.

Yes, the devil may try to stop you from discovering the wonderful benefits of praise, even in this area of sleep. For example, he may try to bring the cares and worries of the day to your mind and try to bombard your mind with fear. But if you will just keep praising God in the midst of every problem and dilemma, God will cause you to rise above your fear and anxiety, and the devil *will* flee!

If you have had difficulty sleeping at night, try making it a habit to praise God, and you'll find it will become easier and easier for you to go to sleep at night. You'll be *praising* yourself to sleep.

Your praise doesn't have to be loud to be effective. You can praise the Lord quietly to yourself so no one is disturbed. Just lay there quietly and praise the Lord and drift off to sleep in the Spirit of the Lord.

Praise and defeat cannot live in the same house. Heartfelt words of praise to God will lift you from defeat to victory. Praising God will deliver you from sickness to health; from despair to joy; and from bondage to liberty.

Why does praise lift us to new heights in God? Because praise is the language of faith. Praise is the language of victory. Praise is the language of heaven. Praise is the language of believing God with your heart and confessing your faith in Him with your mouth. The

Bible says whatever you believe in your heart will eventually come out of your mouth (Matt. 12:34).

A positive praise life requires diligence and boldness. In other words, *you* — not God — determine whether or not you live a life of praise and victory. Victory follows praise. Therefore, since praising God is crucial to gaining the victory in every circumstance of your life, *you* determine whether or not you live a life of despair or a life of praise and victory.

Actually, you find out how close you really live to God and just how much you believe His Word by what comes out of your mouth. For example, when your first reaction to an adverse circumstance is "Praise the Lord!" the praise in your heart just automatically flows out of your mouth.

It's not that you're trying to consciously "put on" something, but praise is just a natural expression of your heart. And the praises of God just automatically and almost unconsciously come from deep inside your heart or spirit.

I'm not talking about praising God at inopportune times and in such a way as to draw attention to yourself and make a spectacle of yourself. Of course, there's a time and place for all things. But if I happen to say, "Praise the Lord!" and I'm around other people, I don't even try to explain it to them, and I certainly don't feel ashamed of it! I'm not ashamed of praising the Lord.

But on the other hand, I'm not going to get on the street corner and make a spectacle of myself either. But if the praises of God just naturally come out of my mouth, I'm not going to make excuses for it either, or be ashamed of it.

You'll find so often that when you have victory in your heart, praise automatically comes out of your mouth. On the other hand, when every circumstance is against you, *if you will praise God by faith, the victory will soon be in your heart!*

Sweet-Smelling Savour

PSALM 34:1-3
1 I will bless the Lord at all times: his praise shall continually be in my mouth.
2 My soul shall make her boast in the Lord: the humble shall hear thereof, and be glad.
3 O magnify the Lord with me, and let us exalt his name together.

2 CORINTHIANS 2:15
15 For we are unto God a sweet savour of Christ. . . .

The praises of the saints are like a sweet-smelling savor as they ascend into the Presence of our Heavenly Father. And if you want to release the power of God to work in your behalf, learn the secret of the *sacrifice* of praise; that means praising God even when you don't *feel* like it.

If you would tap into the power source of praise, you would find yourself enjoying life to the fullest because praise brings you into new dimensions of God's grace.

God is the same God today as He was in the Old Testament. The wonders and miracles He performed for the children of Israel, He can still perform today. We have an untapped power source in the power of praise. We need to learn the power of praise.

If the devil has kept any truth from the Church, it is the secret of the power of praise! He has kept believers from understanding what their rights and privileges are in Christ, and that one way we appropriate God's blessings are by our praise and thanksgiving *in faith* before we see the answer. But in our day and age the Church is beginning to get over into the edge of tapping into the wonderful blessing praising God provides the believer.

> **PSALM 107:21,22**
> **21 Oh that men would praise the Lord for his goodness, and for his wonderful works to the children of men!**
> **22 And let them sacrifice the sacrifices of thanksgiving, and declare his works with rejoicing.**

The lack of praise and thanksgiving is a spirit of the last days. Satan can throttle the power and moving of the Spirit of God if he can shut down praise and thanksgiving because of the power released in praise! The Church of the Lord Jesus Christ has yet to see what will happen when they consistently tap into the wonderful power of God that is released in praise and worship.

Chapter 4
Praise Releases
Your Faith to God

*O Praise the Lord, all ye nations: praise him, all ye
people.*

*For his merciful kindness is great toward us: and the
truth of the Lord endureth for ever. Praise ye the Lord.*

— Psalm 117:1,2

Time and time again we find the psalmists exhort-
ing us to praise the Lord and to give thanks to God.
Why does God's Word exhort His people to praise and
thank Him for His benefits? Because God knows that
praise releases our faith to God.

*"O give thanks unto the Lord; for he is good: because
his mercy endureth for ever"* (Ps. 118:1). We can never
thank God enough because He is good and His mercy
endures forever. How long does God's mercy endure?
Forever! How long is forever? Our finite minds can't
grasp that, but we do know forever will at least be as
long as we will need it to be!

Praise also brings us directly into contact with our
Heavenly Father because the Bible says God inhabits
the praises of His people (Ps. 22:3).

God Inhabits the Praises of His People

PSALM 22:3
**3 But thou art holy, O thou that INHABITEST the
praises of Israel.**

The psalmist is telling us a vital truth in this verse, and one that the Body of Christ cannot afford to neglect. If the Body of Christ really understood what this verse said, we would all be praising the Lord continually because God inhabits the praises of His people.

If God inhabited the praises of Israel because they were His people, how much more does God inhabit the praises of His born-again people! We are certainly God's people too!

If you want to bring the Presence and the power of God into your midst to change any circumstance or any situation you're facing in life, begin to praise God continually from your heart.

Praise is an important principle the Body of Christ has neglected because believers haven't fully understood that God *inhabits* our praises. Therefore, if you praise God in the midst of a test or trial, His power will change that situation. He will work it out for you because God inhabits or indwells praise! And where God is, there is victory!

Our Bodies Are the Temple of God

LUKE 24:53
53 And [the disciples] **were continually in the temple, praising and blessing God. . . .**

You remember that under the Old Covenant, the Presence of God was kept shut up in the Holy of Holies. In the Book of Acts the disciples went to the temple to praise and worship God, because as far as they knew at that time, that was where the Presence of God was. So that's where the disciples went to praise God.

You see, the revelation of the New Testament had not yet been given; Jesus had just been crucified and had been raised from the dead to be seated at the right hand of God the Father. But the revelation that our bodies are the temple of the living God had not yet been revealed. This truth had not yet been revealed and unveiled to the Church.

1 CORINTHIANS 3:16
16 Know ye not that ye are the TEMPLE of God, and that the Spirit of God dwelleth in you?

If you've been born again, you are a new creature in Christ. And if you accept Jesus Christ as your Savior, the Bible promises that God will make His home *in* you: *". . . we will come unto him, and make our abode with him"* (John 14:23).

When we are born again, our bodies become the temple of God, so we don't have to go to a building or a sanctuary before we can worship God. Yes, we are to assemble together in the house of the Lord because the Bible exhorts us not to forsake the assembling of ourselves together (Heb. 10:25).

But we do not have to wait until we get into a church building before we can praise God. *We* are God's temple; we can praise and worship God anywhere *we* are! Furthermore, the Bible says we are to bless the Lord at *all* times — that means *wherever* we may be.

PSALM 34:1
1 I will bless the Lord AT ALL TIMES: his praise
shall continually be in my mouth.

In order for the praise that comes out of our mouths
to be pleasing to God, we need to be sure our praises
come from our hearts and not just from our heads.
Whatever we do for the Lord should come from a heart
of reverence and love toward God.

'Lip Service' or Genuine Praise?

For example, the reason faith confessions are not
working for many Christians is that some people's confessions have become little more than an outward
fleshly exercise; they are just giving the Lord "lip service."

Some Christians quote their confessions by rote or
simply as a *mental* exercise every morning. Their heart
or their spirit is not involved in their confessions in any
way, shape, form, or fashion. They're just quoting scriptures mechanically from their head and not from their
heart.

Faith confessions such as this are little more than a
rote natural or *mental* exercise. Mechanical confessions
that have ceased coming from the heart of man won't
profit much because they are no longer an expression of
the faith that man has in his *heart* toward God.

ROMANS 10:9,10
9 That if thou shalt confess with thy mouth the
Lord Jesus, and shalt BELIEVE in THINE HEART
that God hath raised him from the dead, thou

shalt be saved.
10 For with the HEART man BELIEVETH unto
righteousness; and with the mouth confession is
made unto salvation.

MARK 11:23,24
23 For verily I say unto you, That whosoever shall
say unto this mountain, Be thou removed, and be
thou cast into the sea; and shall not doubt in his
HEART, but shall believe that those things which
he saith shall come to pass; he shall have whatso-
ever he saith.
24 Therefore I say unto you, What things so ever
ye desire, when ye pray, *BELIEVE* that ye receive
them, and ye shall have them.

Nowhere in Scripture will you find that the Bible tells the believer to simply quote mechanical "faith" confessions. The Scriptures specifically mention believing with the *heart* and confessing with the *mouth* (Rom. 10:9,10; Mark 11:23,24).

If the heart or spirit of man is involved, confession is a *spiritual* experience; if only the mouth is involved, confession becomes a mechanical *mental* exercise. We continually need to guard ourselves from getting over into the mental realm with the things of God.

I'm going to make another statement that might surprise you. Do you read the Word of God from a heart of reverence toward God because you love Him and His Word, or do you just read it out of a sense of duty as something you are required to do? If you read the Word with the attitude, *I must read so many chapters in the Word today, so I'll just hurry up and read them!* you're wasting your time. You will gain little from God's Word with that attitude.

Do You Give Only To Receive?

It's much the same way with giving. In other words, the attitude with which you give is important, whether it be your money, your time, or your talents. Some people give to get, and they're never going to receive from God because the attitude of their heart is wrong. We are to desire to give because God has so graciously blessed us, and we are to give out of a heart that desires to bless others.

When your only motive in giving is to receive a blessing for yourself, you're giving with the wrong attitude. Don't ever give just to get. Certainly, you can claim God's promises for giving when your attitude is right, and God's Word will work for you. But don't give for the purpose of being blessed; give to bless others.

When I give, I make it a practice to say to God, "Lord, I thank You that the Word of God is going to work on my behalf because I'm giving in obedience to Your Word. But even if the scriptures didn't promise me a return on my giving, I would still give to You, Father. I'm giving to *You* because of all *You* have done for me."

Do you see the difference? It's the motive of heart that's important to God. One motive is to be a blessing to others out of gratitude to God, and the other motive is simply to selfishly receive more blessings for oneself.

There's a fine line between giving with the right motive, and giving simply to reap a blessing. As in all things, there is a fine line that exists and it has to do with *motive*. That fine line exists in everything we do, and to be pleasing to God we must always maintain the right motives.

Satan, the enemy of our soul, would love to push us over that line, so to speak, and get us to do things with the wrong attitude and motive. But no matter how much God wants to bless us, we cannot receive from Him if our attitudes and motives aren't right.

One benefit we receive from praise is that as we spend time with our Heavenly Father, those impure motives and wrong attitudes will go!

God's Mercy Endures Forever

Praise also releases the power of God on our behalf. *"Praise ye the Lord . . . for his mercy endureth for ever . . ."* (Ps. 106:1). I have heard those words from my father, Rev. Kenneth E. Hagin since I was a child.

When I was growing up, we didn't know some of the principles in God's Word which we now understand about God desiring to meet our needs. And sometimes in financially tight situations when it looked like everything was going wrong and we weren't going to make it, I've seen my dad just look up toward heaven and say, "Praise You, Lord, for Your mercy endures forever," and just go right on down the road like nothing was wrong.

My dad has demonstrated a life of praise even when circumstances looked bleak. And through his life of praise, I have seen the power of God released in our lives in supernatural ways. *The power of God is released through praise.*

Parents know what it's like when their children praise or thank them for a blessing. Our Heavenly Father is our *God*, but He is also our *Father*. I believe when His children begin to praise Him with sincere hearts, He opens the windows of heaven, so to speak, to meet their needs, simply because they are praising Him with right motives.

Praise is proper; it is good and right to praise God and give Him the glory due His Name.

PSALM 113:3:
3 From the rising of the sun unto the going down of the same the Lord's name is to be praised.

This scripture indicates that from the time the sun rises until it goes down — from morning until night — we are to praise the Name of the Lord. That's talking about an *attitude* of praise, isn't it? Our lives should reflect a *lifestyle* of praise! In olden days, everyone woke up when the sun came up and went to bed when the sun went down. Therefore, this scripture is telling us to praise the Lord all day long.

Praise is the easiest way to remove mountains and overcome difficulties. Praise will get your eyes off the *conflict* and onto the *Conqueror*. When you feel depressed, despondent, or downhearted, that's the time to praise the Lord: *"Praise ye the Lord . . . for his mercy endureth for ever"* (Ps.106:1).

Praise lifts us up to another dimension in God's

grace where our attention is no longer focused on the *dilemma*, but on our *Deliverer*, the Lord Jesus Christ. The problem with most of us is that we've got our attention on our circumstances or on the test or trial we're in. But our help comes from God, so He's the One we need to look to — not at the circumstances.

Defeat comes when we continually focus our gaze and attention on the *circumstances*. For example, when Peter was walking toward Jesus on the water and got his eyes off Jesus and onto the circumstances — the wind and the waves loudly clamoring round about him — that's when Peter began to sink (Matt. 14:30). But as long as Peter kept his eyes on the Lord, it didn't make any difference what was happening around him — Peter couldn't fail!

When you release your situation to Jesus, praise will help keep your eyes focused on Him, the Master of *every* situation, and keep your eyes off the circumstances. When your eyes are fixed on the Master of every situation, there is no way you can fail!

Praise Helps Keep the Flesh in Check

I used to play golf occasionally, and sometimes if I made a bad shot, I'd lose my temper. I knew that wasn't pleasing to the Lord, and I soon discovered how I could overcome that. Instead of becoming angry every time I made a bad shot, I began to sing praises to the Lord!

After I learned to do this, instead of getting angry, I would walk off the tee from time to time singing,

"What a Friend We Have in Jesus," or just singing praises to God.

Praise helped me keep my temper in check and my flesh under the dominion of my spirit. If you're having a problem with anger, the next time you notice your temper beginning to flare up, start praising God. Praising God is one way to keep the flesh under the dominion of your spirit.

Praising God helps us overcome negative emotions that may try to dominate us. Praising God helps our spirits stay in control instead of our flesh or our emotions taking over and dominating. Praise gets our eyes on Jesus, and then Jesus can deliver us out of the circumstance. And when you spend time praising God, you'll usually discover that the problem which seemed so big, soon fades away in the light of God's Presence.

Praising God in the midst of any situation encourages our faith and causes us to be able to rise above any situation or circumstance, no matter what it is. Praise keeps us from getting ensnared in the complexities of the problem and helps us get caught up in God instead!

For example, sometimes you have to stand in faith for your answer for a period of time; the solution does not always manifest in a day, a week, or in a month. You have to stand in faith, not looking to the right or to the left at the circumstances, but only straight ahead to God. Praise enables you to be able to take that strong stance of faith and *stay* in faith as you believe God for your answer.

When you're standing in faith believing God for the

answer to your petition, that's when it's easy to get bogged down in the circumstances. When your answer doesn't manifest right away, it's easy to panic and think God hasn't heard you or He isn't working on your behalf.

For example, if you don't have any money, it's easier to see all the bills than it is to see the promises of God! But between the time you pray and the time you see your answer — do *not* relax your faith! God is working in your behalf even though you may not *see* any evidence of it. That's the time to praise God because it releases the power of God to work in a greater measure in your behalf!

When you learn how to praise God in every situation, in every test, and in every trial, it will strengthen your faith in God's Word. Romans 4:20,21 says that Abraham was strengthened in faith *as* he gave praise and glory to God! Praise will keep your eyes on the Author and the Finisher of your faith (Heb. 12:2).

Also, standing on God's Word and praising Him for your victory before you see your answer is the only real solution for weakness and anxiety. Be sure you have hidden the Word of God in your heart, because the Bible says faith comes by hearing, and hearing by the Word of God (Rom. 10:17). The only way you will have faith to stand your ground is by hearing the Word and meditating on the Word, and by hiding it in your heart — your spirit.

Then once you've hidden God's Word in your heart, begin to speak the Word and praise God that He is the

strength of your life (Ps. 27:1). And He will see you
through. Praise God that with God on your side who
can be against you (Rom. 8:31). Drawing nigh to God in
trust and confidence in His Word and with true praise
from your heart, is the only real solution to those feelings of anxiety and weakness we all experience from
time to time.

Your praise to God will turn your sadness to glad-
ness, your defeat to victory, your weakness to strength,
and your trials to triumphs.

> **PSALM 43:5**
> 5   Why art thou cast down, O my soul? and why
> art thou disquieted within me? hope in God: for I
> shall yet praise him, who is the health of my coun-
> tenance, and my God.

The Praise Walk

Learn to walk every day in the life of praising God.
Walking in the praise life is walking in victory. Don't let
a day go by that you don't lift your voice in praise to the
Lord: ". . . *his praise shall continually be in my mouth*"
(Ps. 34:1). Also, praising God is being a doer of the
Word (James 1:22), and the Bible says the doer of the
Word shall be blessed in his deeds (James 1:25).

Consider something else: Jesus already defeated the
enemy at the Cross of Calvary. The victory has already
been won for you in every circumstance, every trial, and
in every test you will ever face in life. The Bible says,
"*Praise waiteth for thee, O God . . .*" (Ps. 65:1). In other
words, it's now up to *you* by your praise to cause the

victory Jesus already won for you on Calvary to manifest in every area of your life!

Determine to praise the Lord at all times and in all situations, knowing that the praises of your mouth bring the triumph of success you've been waiting for. Actually, your praise and your obedience to God's Word determine whether you attain your goals in life and just how far down the road to success in God you're going to be able to go.

Do you want success? Do you want healing? Do you want victory? Do you want your needs to be met? Do you want your heart's desire from God? Begin to praise and magnify God for His greatness and His goodness to you, and for His faithfulness to His Word *instead* of magnifying your problem. Begin to praise God because He has already granted you your inheritance in Christ.

As you begin to praise and thank God for the provisions in His Word, the blessings you desire from God will become a reality in your life, and you will see them come to pass in front of your eyes!

Praising God allows Him to turn your weaknesses into strength, and your failures into triumph. It's up to you. It's not up to God, because God already sent Jesus to defeat the enemy. Satan *is* a defeated foe.

That's why your victory is now up to you because Jesus already won it for you at the Cross. But now you must appropriate God's Word for yourself. Now your own mouth determines whether or not you receive your victory (Deut. 30:11-14,19; Rom. 10:6-8). Purpose in your heart to fill your mouth continually with praises to God.

Praise Brings Joy

The Christian is not to be dominated by his feelings. But on the other hand, when you start praising God, the joyful feelings come and your spirit is encouraged. There's something about praising God that turns the power of God loose on the inside of you, and the joy of the Lord begins to bubble up on the inside.

Outward circumstances do not cause joy; joy comes from within. And the Bible says the joy of the Lord is your *strength* (Neh. 8:10). Praise releases the joy of the Lord in your life. And that joy begins on the inside in your spirit and flows all the way through to the outside where it shows up on your face!

Have you ever experienced the joy of singing songs of praise to the Lord? If you don't know a song of praise, God will give you one by His Spirit. You'll find that as you're praising God, many blessings will begin to happen *through* you, *in* you, and *to* you!

The Body of Christ has not yet tapped into this wonderful resource and benefit the power of praise releases in our lives! We think we've entered into realms of God's power and glory, but really we've just barely begun to enter into all that God has for us on this earth.

I don't believe the Body of Christ has fully understood the power praise releases into the believer's life. If believers realized it, I believe they would be praising God morning, noon, and night!

For example, when the enemy comes against us like

a flood, if we learn to praise God, we'll find Satan will run from us as in terror (James 4:7). Satan already knows he's a defeated foe, but sometimes we act like we don't know it! And there is nothing that will send Satan fleeing faster and bring the angelic host and the power of God on the scene quicker than praising God!

If you want a closer, more intimate relationship with God, learn to praise God at all times. It doesn't matter what your situation is, praise brings you into the realm where by faith you see God at work in your behalf. And praise ushers you into the Presence of God, and doubt, unbelief, depression and fear have to flee when you come into *God's* Presence!

Sometimes people say, "But I can't praise God anytime I want to! I can't praise Him at work." But the lifestyle of praise I'm talking about doesn't require you to necessarily praise God with a loud voice, or at times, to even praise Him out loud at all.

Yes, sometimes it helps just to get alone with God, and loudly and boldly proclaim His praise. Sometimes it is good just to go off by yourself somewhere and yell at the top of your voice, "PRAISE GOD FOR HIS MERCY ENDURETH FOREVER!" But you can also praise God in your heart and never utter a word. You can be in the midst of a crowd of people joyfully praising God in your heart, without anyone knowing about it.

You can have victory in your life such as you have never experienced, if you will take God at His Word and begin to praise Him in advance for the answers you need!

The Bible: Our Praise Book

The Word of God is our praise book. The reason many Christians don't know how to praise God is they don't know what's in *the Book*.

For example, some Christians don't know what's in the Bible because they spend all their time listening to tapes and they're not reading the Bible! Christian teaching tapes are fine, but tapes will never replace reading the Word of God for yourself.

Nothing can take the place of getting God's Word in your *heart* for yourself by careful study and meditation and by fellowshipping with God in His Word.

The psalmist said, *"Thy word have I hid in my heart, that I might not sin against thee"* (Ps. 119:11). It's almost impossible to hide the Word in your heart unless you read the Word of God. You're not going to be able to adequately hide the Word in your heart just by listening to it on tape.

You can retain some of the Word that way, but listening to the Word on tape will never take the place of reading the Word for yourself. And if you read the Bible *and* actively quote it, you retain more of God's Word than if you just passively listen to it on tape.

Educators tell us that you retain more by what you *see* with your eyes and then *say* with your mouth, than you do just by what you *hear* with your ears. In fact, teachers are now finding that an effective way to instruct younger children is to show them a word, and then teach them to sound it out by syllables. That way the children see it, say it, and the word becomes indelibly stamped on that wonderful God-given "computer" God has given to each of us — the brain.

So if you want to discover how to praise God more effectively, read the Word of God for yourself. Meditate in God's Word and sow it into your heart.

> **2 CORINTHIANS 2:14**
> **14 Now thanks be unto God which always causeth us to triumph in Christ, and maketh manifest the savour of his knowledge by us in every place.**

The Scriptures encourage our hearts, and even show us *what* we are to thank God for! Thanks be to God who *always* causes us to triumph — not just some of the time, not just on a part-time basis, but *always*! God always causes us to triumph in Christ!

> **1 CORINTHIANS 15:57**
> **57 But thanks be to God, which giveth us the VICTORY through our Lord Jesus Christ.**

Are you encountering impossible situations and circumstances in your life? Are there mountains you can't get over and impossibilities you can't go around? This verse promises you the victory regardless of the circumstance!

Because you know what God's Word has to say, you can march through life victoriously singing the praises of God. Find out *what* the Word says to you and about you, so *you* can say what the Word says!

1 JOHN 5:4
4   For whatsoever is born of God OVERCOMETH the world: and this is the VICTORY that overcometh the world, even our FAITH.

The enemy, Satan, stalks this land as the god of this world (2 Cor. 4:4). The Bible says Satan goes to and fro as a roaring lion, seeking whom he may devour (1 Peter 5:8). Satan doesn't care what your name is or who you are or what you do. He is out to destroy and devour whomever he can (John 10:10).

Sad to say, Satan devours too many Christians because they don't know who they are in Christ and what their rights and privileges are as joint-heirs with Christ. The devil has rocked others to sleep in the cradle of self-complacency; they have become satisfied with what they have and where they are in God.

Oh, they've talked about what the Lord has done for them, but when you ask them when they last experienced victory in God and the joy of living for Jesus, you find out it was a very long time ago!

Press Forward in God

We should continually be experiencing victory in Christ on a daily basis. And actually, we should forget about the past, both the good and the bad, so we can concentrate on pressing forward toward the mark of the high calling of God in Jesus Christ (Phil. 3:14)! Yes, use your past victories in God as a memorial to continually remind you of God's ability to deliver you. But then press forward to fresh victories in Christ.

There's no time to rest on your past laurels and triumphs. Don't stop to have a victory celebration now, because while you're having a victory celebration, the devil is going to be planning his next attack! We are in a battle in this life, but thank God we know Satan is already a defeated foe, and we have been given the victory in every circumstance in Christ.

Let's not stop to celebrate our victories and in so doing cease to press forward to new victories in Christ. Certainly, we need to praise God with a heart full of gratitude for the victories He's given us, but then keep on going forward in Christ!

The day will come for celebration parties. But let's just keep on praising God and taking more of the devil's territory because one of these days, God the Father is going to look over at His Son, the Lord Jesus Christ, and He's going to say, "Son, go bring My children home!"

1 THESSALONIANS 4:16,17
16 For the Lord himself shall descend from heaven with a shout, with the voice of the archangel and with the trump of God: and the dead in Christ shall rise first:
17 then we which are alive and remain shall be caught up together with them in the clouds. . . .

In *that* day, we are going to have a victory celebration! Then we can pause long enough to celebrate!

Don't slow down in your walk with the Lord. Don't

slow down in your taking ground for the Lord and setting the captives free. Just keep on praising God and pressing forward! Don't ever slow down in your walk with the Lord because the enemy is seeking whom he may devour. And frankly, those who stop to pat themselves on the back are easy prey, and an easy target for Satan's attack!

Besides, too many times while we Christians stop to pat one another on the back and share our victories with one another, Satan is busy trying to destroy our brethren and take the world to hell. Bless God, we don't have time to have victory parties down here! We need to reach the lost! Those who are without God are dying in sin. The world desperately needs to hear the gospel of the Lord Jesus Christ preached. That's what this life is all about in the first place.

Thank God for the prosperity and the many benefits God has bestowed upon us. Thank God for our covenant rights and our redemption in Christ. Thank God, He's healed our bodies and set us free. That's part of the gospel. But we were also born again and put in the family of God to glorify God *and* to go out and win souls into the kingdom of God! We need to be about our Father's business!

Take that same faith you learned to receive prosperity or healing, and begin to praise God and believe for people to be won into the Kingdom. Exercise your faith for people to come into the Kingdom of God. That's the real blessing of this Christian life!

God's heart is for people! Thank God for all of the

benefits He so graciously bestows on us! I believe God desires to prosper His people (3 John 2). I will never believe God wants His children to be in lack and poverty and in pain. That's not the gospel! But my soul stirs to go out and take the devil's kingdom by force to set the captives free and bring people into the Kingdom of God!

God's Delivering Power

You may never have experienced God's delivering power in the midst of adverse circumstances. But you *will* experience it as you begin to praise God with your whole heart and stand firmly upon His Word. The deliverance you have sought from God for so long *will* come as you diligently seek God's face and give Him glory and praise and honor. Those deep desires God has placed in your heart *will* come into manifestation as you begin to enter into God's Presence with His Word and with praise for Him on your lips.

For some of you, the blessings of God are just waiting for your praise — your demonstration of faith in God and His Word. God is trying to get you to shift your focus from the problem to *Him!* Some of you have hardened your heart because of the trying circumstances that have tried to beset you, and you've almost given up. But as you tap into the wonderful power of praising God, the blessings of God will be released to your life in abundance.

Chapter 5
Obtaining the Full Measure
of God's Blessing

If someone told you praising God was a key to
receiving increased blessings in your life, would you
begin to praise God consistently on a continual basis?

I think all of us would, and yet that is exactly what
the Bible tells us. For one thing, the Bible says God
inhabits the praises of His people (Ps. 22:3). Therefore,
if you get God on the scene, no matter what you're
going through, you'll have the power of God manifested
in your life. Wherever the praises of God abound, God's
Presence abounds — and joy and victory.

Praise is a key to receiving increased blessings
poured out in our lives. I'm not suggesting that praise is
a way to manipulate God into giving us what we want
in life. Praise is *not* a method of flattering God so He
will give us what we want.

But praise is a lifestyle, demonstrating your continual trust in your Heavenly Father. Because you trust
God, you believe that what He promised you, He is also
able to perform, and you praise Him for it (Rom. 4:21;
Heb. 10:23).

Praising God regardless of circumstances that come
our way is God's means of bringing us increase in every
area of our lives. In praising God for His goodness, we
demonstrate our trust in Him.

Sincere praise flows out of a relationship of trust in
God, and wholehearted praise produces fruitfulness in

our lives.

Also, we saw in Second Chronicles 20:1-25 that
praise is an *offensive* weapon against the enemy when
Satan tries to come against our lives. Praise also puts
us in a position to receive from God all He has for us
because *praise is an expression of faith.* Praise is the
language of faith!

I am convinced that as we spend quality time fellowshipping with God and praising Him just for who He
is, we will find we have more answers to our prayers
with less struggle and effort! I'm also convinced if we
would spend more time praising God, we would spend
less time praying over and over again about the same
situations in our lives.

Think about it: As long as we're praying in line with
God's Word, we know God hears us because that's what
the Word says. And the Bible also assures us that if we
know God hears us, then we know we have the petition
we desire of Him (1 John 5:14,15). And if we know God
hears our petition, all we need to do is praise Him for
the answer!

You can actually hinder your faith by praying over
and over again about the same situation in an attitude
of doubt and unbelief, as if God did not hear you the
first time. Stay in faith when you pray! Praise helps to
keep you in faith.

I believe if we live a life of praise to God, God will
increase our prayer "fruit" — our answers to prayer.
God is able to increase our results in prayer because
praising God for the answer before we see it is *faith in*

action (Heb. 11:1). Faith is what moves God (Heb. 11:6)! Therefore, living a life of praise is really living a life of faith!

Praise Produces Fruit

I believe Christians have failed to realize the benefits and the fruit that praising God will bring into their lives. We have failed to realize the power of God that is released into our lives when we sincerely praise Him.

Praising God actually allows Christians to utilize or appropriate by faith what already belongs to them in Christ because it releases God's power to work in our behalf. Praise releases God's power to manifest directly to us.

> **PSALM 67:5,6**
> **5   Let the people praise thee, O God; let all the people PRAISE THEE.**
> **6   THEN shall the earth YIELD HER INCREASE; and God, even our own God, shall bless us.**

Why does the psalmist say the earth will yield increase and God will bless us? Increase comes as a result of a life of praise! Praise recognizes and gives God the credit and glory even before the answer is manifested in the natural realm. Praise lays hold of the answer in the spiritual realm and receives the answer from God before it is perceived by the natural man (1 Cor. 2:14).

If you need an increase in your life, begin to praise

God! That's what this verse is saying: *"THEN shall the earth yield her INCREASE . . ."* (Ps. 67:6). Sincere praise moves God. Praise cannot be used as a mechanical "gimmick" to manipulate God, but when it comes from your heart, praise moves God because you're demonstrating your faith in Him!

Psalm 67:6 is saying that no matter what your endeavors are on this earth or whatever you have set your hand to, as you sincerely praise God and put Him first in your life, God will make those things which concern you, prosper *for* you.

If you need an increase in your life of any kind — spiritual, material, emotional, physical, or social — begin to set aside time to seek God and put His Word first. Then begin to praise God as an act of love and trust in Him as your loving Heavenly Father who hears and answers your prayers.

In the Old Testament when these verses were penned, the psalmist was giving the children of Israel a solution to their problems. Notice the Israelites weren't told they wouldn't have any more problems or difficulties. But they were told that God is the One who grants deliverance in times of trouble and increase in times of lack, no matter what the situation!

Psalm 67:6 doesn't indicate that you won't have mountains that will try to hinder you in life and keep you from what God has for you. But it does indicate that when the people of God sincerely praise Him, the earth must grant an increase!

If mountains are in the way hindering that increase

from coming to you, then those mountains must move aside by the power of God which is released by your faith in God's Word and by your praise! If you're walking in obedience to God's Word, praise will move mountains in your life!

God Is a Big God

God is a big God. He is not thwarted from blessing His children no matter what is happening in the world. For example, just because our economy is not what it should be, God can still grant us a financial increase! When we learn to trust God and praise Him regardless of what we see in the natural, God can give us an increase, no matter what circumstances may be standing in our way.

God is not dependent upon *natural* circumstances in order to bless you; He moves in the *supernatural* realm! God can use anything He wants to in order to bring you a financial blessing, if you will just praise *Him* instead of looking to other things as your source. God alone is your Source.

I believe if the people of God would praise God out of a relationship of trust, God could change their financial situation, and make the earth yield an increase to them — no matter what is going on economically in the world.

You hear people complain all the time, "It looks like the dollar is dropping in value again. What are we going to do now?" "Our trade deficit is so great we can't make it financially."

If we're not careful, we can get caught up speaking negative words that can work against us — instead of focusing on God who can provide anything for us. God alone is our Source.

I'm not saying we shouldn't recognize the facts as they exist in the world. But God is greater than any natural facts! God is our Source, and when we praise Him, we put our focus on Him rather than worrying about the problem. With all our attention on Him and on His Word, God can abundantly provide for us — even if He has to create a miracle!

In the Old Testament when God told the children of Israel to praise Him, their problems still loomed like giants before them. And many times their problems were literal giants! But God told them to praise Him and not to be *moved* by their problems — or by those giants; they were only to be moved by God.

One way to get to the place where all your attention is focused on God instead of on your problem is by praising and worshipping God for who *He* is. Then God becomes bigger in *your* sight than any problem. He was bigger than your problem all the time, but you can get so overwhelmed by problems that it's hard to keep a proper perspective. Praise causes God to become bigger to you than your problem.

In the Old Testament when the Israelites praised God as they had been instructed, the earth began to do what it was supposed to do — grant an increase to God's people and bless them. And time and time again, their enemies were put to shame before them!

You see, praising God produces an increase in our lives in whatever area we need an increase. Few Christians have realized this. I'm sure many of us have experienced those areas in our lives that have seemed to be resistant to growth or increase. In some of those areas it seems we've continually experienced a "crop failure."

Try as you might, nothing ever seemed to change those situations or the lack of growth or increase. I believe Psalm 67:5,6 addresses those hard-to-produce areas in our lives too.

In other words, even in the hard places — the areas that have resisted change — if we will keep our eyes off the problem and focus only on giving God praise, *God* will cause an increase to come no matter how many crop failures we've had in the past!

There are other areas where we probably all need to experience increase in our lives. For example, each one of us has dreams, desires, gifts, and talents placed inside of us by God. But many of us don't know how to develop our gifts or how to use our talents productively to the glory of God. Many of us have dreams, but we don't know how to practically implement those dreams so they become a reality in our lives.

I believe as we learn to live a life of praising God — I don't mean every once in awhile, but consistently — God will see to it that those areas in our lives bring forth fruit to His glory. The earth and everything we set our hand to must prosper as we put God and His Word first and consistently praise Him for His goodness to us.

Do you want an increase in your life! Then begin to draw closer to God and His Word and give Him praise! No matter where you need an increase in your life — whether it's in finances or in your career or in achieving the potential God has for you — as you praise God from your heart as a lifestyle, whatever you set your hand to must yield its increase to you!

Christians need to learn to tap into the vast storehouse of treasure to be found in sincere, heartfelt praise to God! Much awaits them as they will begin to press into this dimension of God's grace, and see for themselves the joy that is released in their lives!

Not Only Increase, But Blessings!

PSALM 67:5,6
5   Let the people PRAISE THEE, O God; let all the people PRAISE THEE.
6   THEN shall the earth yield her INCREASE; and GOD, even our own God, SHALL BLESS US.

Let's look at these verses again. Two important statements are made in verse 6. One, as we saw, when we diligently and sincerely praise God for His goodness to us, God will cause us to receive a natural, material *increase* from this world we live in. I believe this increase must come from all of our endeavors — if we're putting God's will and His Word first in our lives.

Two, as we praise God, the *blessings* of God will be upon our lives in abundance. But the blessings of God won't come to us in the fullest measure unless we do what verse 5 says — live a life of praising God!

I don't know of any Christian who doesn't desire the blessings of God. Most of God's children earnestly desire the full measure of God's blessings in their lives.

The Bible tells us in Ephesians 1:3 that we are blessed with all spiritual blessings in heavenly places in Christ, but sometimes it seems that God's children don't know how to tap into what already belongs to them.

Psalm 67:5 and 6 tell us how to do that: *"Let the people praise thee, O God. . . . Then shall the earth yield her increase. . . ."* Praise is one way God's people tap into and appropriate what already belongs to them through Christ. Praise is one way the increase comes!

If God's people would learn the secret of praising God sincerely from their hearts regardless of circumstances, they would find the blessings of God overtaking them! Instead of running after blessings, the blessings of God would run after them *and* overtake them! Then whatever they set their hands to would prosper and their endeavors would yield an increase in every area. God has promised an increase for those who praise Him from a sincere heart!

If you have a need or if you're facing a lack in any area of your life whether it is financial, social, physical, or emotional, no doubt you've prayed and sought God about it. But if you haven't seen your answer manifest yet, instead of praying about your need over and over again in unbelief, just present your petition before God in simple faith. Then begin to praise Him that He has heard you and is answering your petition. That's faith!

Praise confirms to your own heart that God has heard and answered your prayers because according to the Bible, ". . . *What things soever ye desire, when ye pray, believe that ye receive them, and ye shall have them*" (Mark 11:24). In other words, faith isn't faith until you say, "Thank You, Father, I believe I receive my answer *now!*" Praise is that act of believing and receiving by faith.

Praise: Faith's Position

Instead of praying over and over again about the same petition, get in faith and *stay* in faith by praising God for your answer before you *see* your answer! Act like God has already heard you because the Bible says He does hear you when you pray according to His will!

God wants your praise, not because He needs it for Himself, but because He's trying to get you in a position of *faith* so He can answer your prayer. Faith is praising God for the answer before you see it. After praise comes increase, abundance, and the blessings of God running after you and overtaking you in life!

The key to faith is praising God *before* you see your answer. Praise acknowledges that God has heard you and that He is busy answering your prayer. Praise is actively trusting in God, and the Bible promises that whoever trusts in God will not be ashamed (Ps. 25:2). You won't be ashamed if you trust in God and stand

your ground in faith praising God because you will have
your answer!

There's power in praise! The power of God is
released to the believer in praise. But to be effective,
praise must come from the heart and be a lifestyle —
not just a mechanical gimmick used as a means of
escape when we get into trouble. That's not true praise.
True praise flows out of a loving relationship with our
Heavenly Father; we praise God because we love and
trust Him, not because we're trying to manipulate Him
to do something for us.

The Lesson of the Ten Lepers

In the healing of the ten lepers, we get a glimpse of
one of the benefits of praise and thanksgiving.

LUKE 17:11-19
**11 And it came to pass, as he went to Jerusalem,
that he passed through the midst of Samaria and
Galilee.**
**12 And as he entered into a certain village, there
met him ten men that were lepers, which stood
afar off:**
**13 And they lifted up their voices, and said, Jesus,
Master, have mercy on us.**
**14 And when he saw them, he said unto them, Go
shew yourselves unto the priests. And it came to
pass, that, as they went, they were cleansed.**
**15 And one of them, when he saw that he was
healed, turned back, and with a loud voice GLORI-
FIED God.**
**16 And fell down on his face at his feet, giving him
THANKS: and he was a Samaritan.**

17 And Jesus answering said, Were there not ten
cleansed? but where are the nine?
18 There are not found that returned TO GIVE
GLORY TO GOD, save this stranger.
19 And he said unto him, Arise, go thy way: THY
FAITH hath made thee whole.

Ten lepers cried out to Jesus for cleansing. When
you study Bible types, you find that apart from being
an actual disease, leprosy is also a type of sin. In reality, these ten lepers were healed of a literal physical
disease. But we can also say that anyone who has sin in
his life is in need of cleansing by the blood of Jesus.

All ten lepers cried out to Jesus for cleansing. But
only one of the ten lepers returned to Jesus to give
thanks, and Jesus commended him for it. In fact, Jesus
indicated that this leper's praise and thanksgiving had
something to do with his faith making him *whole*.

In other words, verse 14 says all of the lepers were
cleansed, but only one was made *whole*! And he was
made whole after he spent some time in thanksgiving!

PSALM 103:1-4
1 Bless the Lord, O my soul: and all that is within
me, bless his holy name.
2 Bless the Lord, O my soul, and forget not all his
benefits:
3 Who forgiveth all thine iniquities; who healeth
all thy diseases;
4 Who redeemeth thy life from destruction; who
crowneth thee with lovingkindness and tender
mercies.

This leper received an immediate return or reward

from his praise — he was made whole. The phrase, "he was a Samaritan" in Luke 17:16 is significant. In Jesus' day, the Jews and the Samaritans hated each other because the Jews considered the Samaritans a half-breed race.

In fact, rather than take the short way to Jerusalem and go through Samaria, the Jews would walk miles out of their way, simply to avoid passing through Samaria.

However, I imagine it didn't matter to any of these lepers that one of them was a Samaritan because they were *all* covered with leprosy and all they wanted was to be healed and set free.

When people are hurting or they've become social outcasts because of sickness or disease, cultural distinctions become unimportant. Basically, people all over the world have the same need to be healthy and fulfilled in life.

This Samaritan was the only one who came back to give thanks to God — yet in the eyes of society he was an outcast. God doesn't look on man the same way people do. His love knows no limitations. God's love is extended to those whom society has long since disregarded. God will always answer the cry of the one whose heart is hungry, whoever the person may be or whatever his problems may be.

Also, many times when we read the story of the ten lepers and see the ingratitude of the nine who never returned to give thanks to God, we condemn them saying, "Oh, isn't that terrible! Only one of them returned to praise God!" But how many times do *we* as God's own children fall short of praising Him!

Thank God for His Bountiful Blessings!

We must always remember to live in an attitude of thanksgiving to God for His bountiful blessings to us.

Many times new converts are so thrilled to be a part of the family of God, and their praise and gratitude to God is refreshing. They sometimes put those of us who have been born again for some time to shame by their exuberant praise!

For example, one young man was saved in a church service recently, and it was gratifying to see his demonstration of praise and his gratitude to God. His praise was infectious and joyful. He was so grateful to God for his salvation, he kept exclaiming, "I feel like a brand-new person. I feel totally different! I'm brand-new!"

Very often people who have been born again or healed are deeply grateful to God and praise Him continually for His blessings. Yet sometimes it seems those of us who have been saved for many years and have walked under the protective hand of God fail to praise God as we should. It's almost as if we take God's blessings for granted.

Praise Keeps the Channel of Blessing Open

LUKE 19:37
37 And when he [Jesus] was come nigh, even now at the descent of the mount of Olives, the whole

multitude of the disciples began to rejoice and praise God with a loud voice for all the mighty works that they had seen.

A group of Jesus' disciples gathered together to praise God for all the mighty works they had witnessed in Jesus' ministry. The Bible doesn't say exactly what the mighty works were, but we do know that Acts 10:38 says, *"How God anointed Jesus of Nazareth with the Holy Ghost and with power: who went about doing good, and healing all that were oppressed of the devil; for God was with him."*

Evidently these disciples had witnessed some of the mighty works Jesus had done because the Bible says they were praising God for what they had seen.

We need to learn to praise God for what we see happening in our lives and in the lives of our brothers and sisters in Christ. When the power of God is demonstrated in someone else's life, we need to learn how to praise God for it and to rejoice with them.

Sometimes there is a tendency in the natural to be jealous if someone else is being blessed by God more than we think we are. We may even say to ourselves, *Bless God, I've been believing God and praising Him, and I haven't received my answer yet! Why should that person receive his answer?* Even though we don't always voice these attitudes, without saying a word, we often *display* them.

Part of spiritual maturity is learning to praise God no matter what our circumstances are in life — whether we have an abundance or a little. By praising

God when someone else receives from God, you keep the channel of blessing open so you, too, can receive from God. But if you harbor a wrong attitude and think, *Bless God, I should have been the one who got blessed!* you close the door to receive your blessing from God.

Praise Empowers Our Faith

I believe Christians are missing out on the power that is available to them through praise. Many times they don't realize that praise *is* a demonstration of their faith.

Also, Romans 4:20,21 tells us that praise empowers our faith.

> **ROMANS 4:20,21**
> **20** He [Abraham] **staggered not at the promise of God through unbelief; but was strong in faith, giving glory to God;**
> **21 And being fully persuaded that, what he had promised, he was able also to perform.**

Look at the same verse in *The Amplified Bible.*

> **ROMANS 4:20,21 (*Amplified*)**
> **20 No unbelief or distrust made him waver or doubtingly question concerning the promise of God, but he GREW STRONG and was EMPOWERED BY FAITH as he gave PRAISE and GLORY to God.**
> **21 Fully satisfied and assured that God was able and mighty to keep His word and to do what He had promised.**

When your back is against the wall, so to speak, and every circumstance is against your succeeding in life, instead of griping and complaining, begin to praise God and give Him glory. Change your focus!

Faith is a change of focus from the *problem* to *God.* Your focus — what you are giving your attention to — is all-important in succeeding in life. And praise helps you put your focus on God and keep it there!

You'll find that praise is one way God has provided for us to rise above those circumstances in life which sometimes try to press in upon us and keep us down and discouraged. God knows the power that is released into our lives as we praise Him. If we'll begin to actively demonstrate our faith by praising Him, we'll find ourselves on the other side of those seemingly impossible circumstances!

Try Thanksgiving

Many years ago there was a missionary to China who was living in constant defeat because of the overwhelming struggles he faced on the mission field. He prayed and prayed and prayed about his situation, and he repeatedly asked God why he wasn't seeing any results to his missionary efforts. But no answer came. It seemed that depression and discouragement flanked him on every side. Everything he touched seemed to turn to defeat. No answer seemed to come from heaven.

Finally, he decided to leave his mission station and go further into the interior of the country to another

mission station so he could seek God without distrac-
tion. He determined to get on his face before God and
pray until he got an answer.

Does that sound familiar? I've heard people say, "I'm
just going to take off and go to the woods (or the barn or
the mountains or *somewhere*) and pray until I get my
answer!"

When this missionary arrived at the mission station
in China's interior, he walked into the mission station,
and the first thing he noticed was a sign hanging on the
wall that immediately caught his attention. It said,
"Try *thanksgiving.*"

Immediately the Spirit of God spoke to his heart
and told him *that* had been his problem; he had continually prayed over and over about the same situation,
never thanking God for the answer! He had really been
praying in doubt and unbelief. God knew thanksgiving
would get him into faith and *keep* him in faith.

The missionary realized he'd been praying and
praying and asking and asking, but he hadn't been
thanking God at all. In other words, he hadn't even
acknowledged that God had *heard* him, let alone
answered him. All that time he had been praying in
unbelief — not in faith.

The missionary immediately returned to his own
mission station, thrilled with what God had revealed to
his heart. He didn't even spend the night in the interior
at that mission station because he had received his
answer from heaven!

All the way back home, in simple faith he praised

God that God had heard and answered his prayers. As he did, every bit of depression, disappointment, discouragement, and defeat lifted from him. By the time he reached his mission station, he had such revival in his own heart that God used him mightily to bring a major revival to that entire area!

You see, this missionary had known *the power of prayer*, but he realized that he had neglected *the power of praise*. He came to understand the mighty power in praise. *Praising God while the situation still looks bleak is faith!*

God Is Waiting for Your Praise

PSALM 65:1
1   Praise waiteth for thee, O God, in Sion: and unto thee shall the vow be performed.

Many of you are praying and waiting on God for the answer to your petitions. But when you're waiting on God for the answer, wait in an attitude of praise and thanksgiving. Wait in an attitude of expectancy! Wait on God in praise! Wait on God in faith!

Prayer *asks*, but praise *receives*. Praise receives the answer by faith and thanks God for the answer before the answer is actually visible to the natural man. Of course, there is a proper time to exercise both *prayer* and *praise*. Both prayer and praise are necessary and important. But after you've prayed and believed God for the answer based on His Word, that's the time to stay in faith by praising Him.

You can actually get out of faith and into unbelief by praying over and over again about the same petition, if you are praying as if God didn't hear you the first time. Yes, some kinds of prayer such as the prayer of intercession, require diligent prayer over a period of time. But even then you need to stay in faith. Praise ensures that you keep your heart and mind in an attitude of faith; therefore, praise can actually hasten your answer.

There are different kinds of prayer, and all of them are valid in their place. However, the prayer of faith and the prayer of agreement only take a short time to pray when you pray in faith and believe God hears you. You don't have to get into a long theological discourse with God. Just pray simply and pray straight from your heart.

How To Approach Your Heavenly Father

PSALM 100:4,5
4   Enter INTO HIS GATES with thanksgiving, and INTO HIS COURTS with praise: be thankful unto him, and bless his name.
5   For the Lord is good; his mercy is everlasting; and his truth endureth to all generations.

In this verse we find a secret to entering into the Presence of our Heavenly Father. The key word in this verse is "enter." This is an open invitation to the child of God. Go on in to the Presence of God!

Also, the understood subject of the sentence is "You." *You* are to enter into God's gates and into His courts with praise. You don't need someone else to do your praying for you. *You* are to come before your Heavenly Father with thanksgiving and praise. Take this verse for *yourself* and enter into God's Presence.

Another key in this verse is that you are to enter your Heavenly Father's Presence with *thanksgiving* — whether you feel like it or not! Even if you don't have a penny in your pocket, you can still enter into His courts with thanksgiving. Whether you are happy or sad or feel good or feel bad, enter into your Heavenly Father's Presence.

> **HEBREWS 4:16**
> **16 Let us therefore come BOLDLY unto the throne of grace, that we may obtain mercy, and find grace to help in time of need.**

We are all familiar with Hebrew 4:16 which invites us to come boldly before the throne of grace. The child of God is invited to come boldly to God without fear or condemnation because God is our Heavenly Father. But we are also to prepare our hearts before we begin to seek God (Ps. 66:18).

No matter how you *feel*, go boldly into your Heavenly Father's Presence. God is waiting for you to come before Him. After you've spent time in His Presence, no matter how needy you were when you came before Him, you'll go away changed and your needs will be met!

Praise Eradicates Selfishness

There's another benefit to entering into God's gates

with thanksgiving and praise. Praise eradicates selfishness in our prayers. In other words, instead of running
into your Heavenly Father's Presence demanding,
"Gimme, gimme, gimme! My name is Jimmy. I'll take
all you'll gimme!" you'll learn to just enjoy being in
God's Presence. Approaching your Heavenly Father
with demands and selfish attitudes will gain you nothing.

No, there is a reason the Bible admonishes us to
enter into God's gates with thanksgiving. The Bible is
telling us what the attitude of our hearts should be as
we approach our Heavenly Father: "Father, I thank and
praise You for what You've done for me. You've delivered me and You've set me free. You've healed my body,
and You've met all of my needs, and I thank You for it."

Also, by praising and thanking God for what He's
done for you and worshipping Him for who He is, you
won't struggle to come into God's Presence. The Bible
says the child of God can approach the throne of God
boldly through the blood of Jesus. And the attitude of
praise and thanksgiving ushers you immediately into
your Heavenly Father's Presence.

Praise and thanksgiving is the proper way to
approach God. God desires to give you your heart's
desire (Ps. 37:4), but He can't answer attitudes of selfishness and arrogance. And after all, we're talking
about entering into the Presence of Almighty God, the
One who created heaven, the earth, and the entire universe! He deserves our praise!

Too many times we may fail to receive answers to

our prayers because we do not have the right heart attitude as we approach our Heavenly Father. Let's learn
what is pleasing to our Heavenly Father and practice
doing that. He is our *Father*, but He is also our *God*!
The problem is most of us don't take time enough to
study the Scriptures to understand what is pleasing to
God and how to come into His Presence properly.

Your Heavenly Father
Looks on Your Heart Attitude

When you were growing up, you probably learned
there was a proper way to approach your earthly father.
And if you approached him the right way, most of the
time you had no problem communicating what you
needed from him and receiving it. But if you went to
him in tones of arrogance or demanding from him what
you wanted, you probably didn't have much success!

In fact, over the years, most of us probably also
learned how to approach teachers, employers, and various other people in our lives to communicate effectively
to them and receive what we needed from them. That's
part of growing up and learning to work with one
another. Those same people probably also learned how
to work with us to help us rise to our full potential and
to excel to the best of our ability.

In much the same way, there is a proper way to
approach God. And if we come before Him with the
right heart attitude, we put ourselves in a position to be
able to receive from Him.

Be Honest With God

When we come before God, we need to talk to Him out of our heart. Instead, many people talk to God like they would their banker. They go to their banker and talk about everything they can think of before they finally get to the subject — the money they need to borrow! They go into a long discourse trying to impress him so they can get their loan!

You don't have to do that with God. If you're born again, He's your Father. You don't have to impress your Heavenly Father. He loves you just the way you are. So when you talk to Him, get right to the point! Don't worry that your words must be exact and theologically "perfect." You can just pour out your heart to Him.

PSALM 62:8
8   Trust in him at all times; ye people, pour out your heart before him: God is a refuge for us. Selah.

When you were a child, did you go to your earthly father with a long, impressive list of your good qualities so he would give you what you needed? No, you probably just walked in and told him what you needed and he responded.

Do the same thing with your Heavenly Father. When you pray, get to the point with Him. Tell Him exactly what you need. Be specific. Tell Him exactly what's on your heart.

Then before you leave His Presence, express your

confidence in Him that He's taken care of this need for you. You do that by praising and thanking Him. When you express your confidence in your Heavenly Father by praising Him, you're acting in faith, and your faith gives God something to respond to.

After all, He promised in His Word that whatever you ask in Jesus' Name according to His will, He would grant you (John 16:23,24). You've got His Word that He will answer you, so act like it! Praise is acting like you believe the promises in God's Word and that you believe God is faithful to His promises.

When you pray, believe the Bible and start praising and thanking God *immediately for your answer.* It's important that you are confident in God and in the integrity of His Word, and that you believe God will be faithful to answer your petition. Praise helps build that confidence because praise affirms to your *own* heart that God is able to meet your need.

Therefore, don't continue to ask God over and over again for the same request. He heard you the first time you prayed! Praise Him, affirming that you *know* He has heard you and that you *know* the answer is on its way!

Sometimes children think in order to get what they want from their parents, they have to wear them down by begging them. We may laugh at that, but when we were children we probably did the same thing.

But with God, you don't have to wear Him down to get an answer to your prayers. His Word says His ears are always open to the cry of the righteous (Ps. 34:15).

That means He hears you the first time you pray. And as long as you're praying in accordance with His Word, you can be assured the answer is on its way — the *first* time you pray. God's character and His integrity to His Word can be depended upon (Heb. 10:23; Heb. 11:11).

However, we do need to understand that our faith will be tested. The test of our faith usually occurs from the time we pray until we see the answer actually manifested. That's usually when Satan will try to hit us with doubt and unbelief and thwart us from receiving *by faith* what we need from God. That's just the time to stand firm in faith by continuing to thank and praise God that the answer is on its way!

Praise Lifts Our Spirits

Praise has the power to lift our spirits and loose us from bondage.

> **PHILIPPIANS 4:4**
> **4 Rejoice in the Lord alway: and again I say, Rejoice.**

Philippians 4:4 doesn't say we are to rejoice when we feel like rejoicing, or that we are to rejoice only when we're on the mountaintop. The Word of God declares that we are to rejoice in the Lord *always*.

Why would God especially instruct us to stay in an attitude of rejoicing, thanksgiving, and praise? Because God knows it's to *our* benefit to stay in an attitude of constant praise! You see, *we* are the ones who benefit when we praise God — we are uplifted, encouraged, and our faith is invigorated when we praise God.

Continually rejoicing and praising God lifts our spirits and causes us to see the test or trial we may be facing from a different perspective — from God's viewpoint. That's one reason God wants us to offer up to Him the *sacrifice* of praise continually.

The sacrifice of praise is praising God when we don't feel like it — and God knows that's exactly *when* we need to praise Him. God knows *we* will benefit from praising Him because it will lift and encourage our spirits to go on in faith in Him.

It's time we learned that praise is a key that will encourage us when we're feeling down or overwhelmed with the pressures of life. Expressing our confidence in God through praise will bring us peace in the midst of any storm. Praise refocuses our gaze *from* the storm *to* God. Praise lifts the heaviest burdens off of our shoulders!

When the pressure is on and you're under great strain, spend extra time waiting on God in an attitude of praise. If you'll be faithful to do this, you'll find that instead of the pressure getting to you, you'll get to the pressure! God wants us to learn to praise Him in the *midst* of the storm while the waves are yet raging — *not* after the storm has already subsided!

Are you facing a crisis in your life? Are you in the "midnight hour" of that trial in your life? Do you need to be delivered out of circumstances that seem impossible and overwhelming to you? Set aside time to come boldly into the Presence of your Heavenly Father with your praises and watch Him deliver you, no matter what you're going through.

Fair Weather Christians

PSALM 113:3
3   From the rising of the sun unto the going down of the same the Lord's name is to be praised.

Too many times we are "fair weather" Christians. We praise the Lord as long as everything is going good — as long as the sun is shining and the path before us is bright. But the Bible tells us it is God's will for us to praise God no matter what we are facing in life.

1 THESSALONIANS 5:18
18 In every thing GIVE THANKS: for this is the will of God in Christ Jesus concerning you.

The Apostle Paul praised God in every situation he encountered in life. We have Paul's own testimony of his life and some of the persecution and major tests and trials he faced. I believe Paul knew what he was talking about when he said under the inspiration of the Holy Spirit that we are to give thanks to God always — in every circumstance. Paul had been there!

Paul learned how to give thanks to God when he was in the most trying of circumstances. For example, Paul was shipwrecked, beaten, thrown in prison, and was stoned and left for dead, yet he continued to praise

God. In all the hard places, Paul praised God.

But it was this attitude of praise that allowed Paul to declare at the end of his life, *"I have fought a good fight, I have finished my course, I have kept the faith: Henceforth there is laid up for me a crown of righteousness . . ."* (2 Tim. 4:7,8). The outcome of such a life of praise is also found in Paul's statement, "He always causes me to triumph in Christ Jesus" (2 Cor. 2:14). Praise brings the victory! Praise brings the triumph!

Give Thanks in Everything

1 THESSALONIANS 5:18
18 IN every thing give thanks: for this is the will of God in Christ Jesus concerning you.

It's important to notice the Bible says we are to give thanks *in* everything, not that we are to give thanks and praise *for* everything. There is a vast difference.

Several years ago, much was written on the subject of praise. As a result, God's people began to experience tremendous results in answered prayer because they were tapping into the power of God that is released through praise.

But according to some of the teaching during that time, we were to thank God *for* the difficulty, problem, test, or trial. That particular teaching was slightly off-base scripturally, and some Christians got off into error because of it.

You see, we are not to praise God *for* the adverse circumstances, *for* the sicknesses, or *for* the calamity, test, or trial Satan sends our way. The Bible doesn't teach that. But the Bible does teach that *in* the midst of every trial or test — no matter what we go through in life — we are to praise God.

In other words, First Thessalonians 5:18 is telling us that no matter what the test or trial, we are to keep our eyes on God, not on the circumstance. God knows praising Him in the midst of the fiery trials will cause our eyes to focus on Him rather than on the problem. And He knows that praising Him, instead of focusing on the trial, unleashes God's power to work in our behalf.

Again, this is not something we do mechanically to try to manipulate God or manipulate circumstances. It is heartfelt praise that moves God, which can only come from a loving relationship with our Heavenly Father.

You need to learn to praise God as a lifestyle regardless of circumstances. Praising God moves you into a position to receive God's best in your life. Praise unleashes the power of God on your behalf. In everything give thanks — not *for* everything. *In* everything go to God with a grateful heart, and praise Him for who *He* is.

In the midst of any test or trial, go to your Heavenly Father and praise Him for His delivering power, and He will make a way of escape! Praise Him that He's bigger than any problem or any trial you may be facing.

The Power of Continual Praise

PSALM 34:1
1 I will bless the Lord at all times: his praise

shall continually be in my mouth.

Many times when I'm driving down the road or working at my office, I just begin to praise the Lord. I don't stop to see who's around, although I don't try to make a spectacle of myself. But on the other hand, I think it's time we aren't intimidated by the world either.

People in the world aren't intimidated about using bad language and telling off-color jokes in our presence! They're not afraid to curse God in front of us! They're not afraid to act any way they want to around us! So we need to learn not to be afraid to praise God. If the world is going to curse Him, then bless God, we can praise Him!

You can praise God when you're going about your ordinary routine. You can praise God when you're working on your car, or when you're running down the length of the basketball court, or when you're driving down the street. You can praise God when you're mowing the lawn or washing the dishes or sweeping the floor. It doesn't matter what you're doing, you can praise God continually!

Praise be unto the Lord God our Father and our Creator. Our lips should be continually expressing the exuberance of joy from our spirits because of what God has delivered us from.

The praises of God are to be continually in our mouths because praise is the answer to many of our problems. That's not to minimize prayer in any way.

But some of our answers are only waiting on our praise for the answer to manifest.

Faith praises God for the answer before the answer is visible to the natural man. Many times praise is the key that unlocks the answers you've long waited for.

We need to learn how to continually speak forth the praises of God from sincere hearts. Praising God shows an *attitude* of an obedient and grateful heart. How speedily God can answer the genuine praise of a grateful heart!

Oh, let us learn to praise God!

PSALM 95:1,2
1 O come, let us sing unto the Lord: let us make a joyful noise to the rock of our salvation.
2 Let us come before his presence with thanksgiving, and make a joyful noise unto him with psalms.

PSALM 32:11
11 Be glad in the Lord, and rejoice, ye righteous: and shout for joy, all ye that are upright in heart.

1 THESSALONIANS 5:16
16 Rejoice evermore.

PSALM 150:6
6   Let every thing that hath breath praise the Lord. . . .

PSALM 92:1
1   It is a good thing to give thanks unto the Lord, and to sing praises unto thy name, O most High.

1 PETER 2:9
9   But ye are a chosen generation, a royal priesthood, an holy nation, a peculiar people; that ye

should shew forth the praises of him who hath
called you out of darkness into his marvellous
light.

Praise God for His Wonderful Works

We have yet to uncover the unlimited source of
God's power through praise.

PSALM 107:21,22
21 Oh that men would praise the Lord for his
goodness, and for his wonderful works to the children of men!
22 And let them sacrifice the sacrifices of thanksgiving, and declare his works with rejoicing.

Have you ever considered that one of God's "wonderful works" to the children of men is our strong, healthy
bodies that function properly! Let's praise God in appreciation and gratitude for what He has given us! And if
we aren't experiencing the fullness of those blessings,
praise God, we can appropriate them by faith in God's
Word.

We have much to praise God for. In fact, when you
think about it, in one sense of the word, we really owe
God a "debt" of praise for everything He's done for us!
The number one reason to praise God is out of gratitude
to Him for our salvation, our redemption.

We have life and have it more abundantly because
of our redemption in Christ (John 10:10). But we also
need to learn to praise God for our health and healing,
which is a part of our redemption. Too often we take our
health for granted. Those who have been healed from a

deathbed illness don't take their health and life for granted! People who have been healed are usually especially grateful for the blessings of good health.

I know in my own life, I frequently thank God for my health, my family, and the blessings He has given me in life. I've always been active in sports, and I'm grateful to God that I have a healthy body which is unhampered by sickness or disease.

I also like to thank God for the simple blessings we believers too often overlook and take for granted. We should praise God every day for the many benefits He provides for us.

God Daily Loads Us With Benefits

PSALM 68:19
19 Blessed be the Lord, who DAILY LOADETH US WITH BENEFITS, even the God of our salvation. Selah.

A friend of mine once related to me that his father had lost the use of both of his hands when my friend was a child. His father had unknowingly grabbed ahold of a live electric wire and both his hands were badly burned.

My friend related that even as a child, he'd had to tie his father's shoes and help him button his shirt because one of his father's hands was burned completely off, and the other one had no feeling in it whatsoever.

When was the last time we praised God for such a

simple blessing as our two hands? We Christians take too much for granted sometimes! We need to praise the Lord for the blessings in life which we are so often apt to overlook or take for granted.

Those of us who are in the ministry need to be thankful to God for the privilege of serving Him in the ministry. Many times as I go to sleep at night, I praise God that He's allowed me to be in the ministry. I also praise God for natural blessings such as a bed to sleep in, food to eat, and a roof over my head.

Many people in the world pillow their heads upon the hard ground and go hungry day after day. Therefore, we should not take the precious blessings of food and shelter for granted. I think the Body of Christ needs to learn to praise God, because we have a Heavenly Father who loves us and desires to provide for us.

If you have a lack or an inability in your life, begin to praise God because God has promised in His Word to meet every one of your needs. If you're oppressed by doubt, unbelief, or fear, begin to declare aloud, "God has not given me a spirit of fear, but of power and of love and of a sound mind" (2 Tim. 1:7). Begin to praise God that you do not have to suffer under the bondage of fear because you are in Christ, and then begin to act like His Word is true because it *is* true!

If you need healing, begin to praise God that by His stripes you are healed (Isa. 53:5; 1 Peter 2:24). That's God's promise to you! Take Him at His Word. Declare what the Word says: "I praise God I am healed by the stripes of Jesus Christ."

Praise Unleashes God's Delivering Power

When you feel you don't have the strength to praise God, praise Him anyway. When you don't feel like praising God, praise Him anyway. That's the "sacrifice" of praise the Bible refers to.

When you don't have any money in your pocket and your bank account is empty, praise God that He is able to meet all of your needs. That's faith! And keep on praising God, because if you're sincere, your heartfelt praise will unleash the power of God in your life so God can manifest Himself to you.

If you need deliverance from a habit that has you bound, use God's Word and bind the power of the enemy over your life according to Matthew 18:18. Then begin to praise God for complete deliverance. If you'll begin to praise God for your deliverance before you *see* any change, you'll find that God's power will be manifested on your behalf.

Overcoming Habits

A man once shared with me the struggle he was having giving up cigarette smoking. He finally requested prayer for deliverance from this habit which had him bound. Then every time he had a desire for a cigarette, he would praise God that he'd been delivered. He told me that every time he praised God, the desire for cigarettes would completely leave him.

Before long, as he faithfully kept praising God, he lost all desire to smoke. After he was delivered, he still kept praising God, only then it was because he was set free from that habit!

Sometimes you may have to stand in faith on God's Word for your complete deliverance to manifest. But if you will diligently thank and praise God for His delivering power and praise Him for the answer, His Word will set you free.

You need to praise God *in* every circumstance, *in* every situation, and *in* every trial. And God will make a way to deliver you from that fiery trial no matter what it is!

If you will praise God consistently in your life with heartfelt praise, the power of God will be made available to work on your behalf in a way you have not yet experienced.

PSALM 45:17
17 I will make thy name to be remembered in all generations: therefore shall the people praise thee for ever and ever.

Praise the Lord in everything you do.
Praise the Lord as you walk down the street.
Praise the Lord as you drive in your car.
Praise the Lord as you go about your daily work.
Praise the Lord and continue to praise the Lord.
Praise the Lord and God will deliver you.
Praise the Lord and the power of God
                    will uplift you.

Praise the Lord and no weapon can stand
　　　　against you.
Praise the Lord and the power of God will set
　　　　your feet to dancing.
Praise the Lord and watch the glory of God
　　　　flood your heart and your life.

PSALM 66:1
1 **Make a joyful noise unto God, all ye lands.**

The Bible says to make a joyful noise unto the Lord.
Praise is making a joyful noise to God. Some Christians
hesitate to make a joyful noise to God because they're
convinced they can't sing a note! But if you sincerely
desire to praise God from your heart, then no matter
what you may think you sound like — to God, it's
praise!

Of course, there's a proper time and place for all
things — including making a joyful noise to God!
Normally, it wouldn't be proper to make a loud joyful
noise in the middle of the pastor's sermon in church!
But when the congregation is praising God, or when
you are alone, then your joyful noise is appropriate!

Begin to make praise a habit and a way of life —
part of your lifestyle. When you get up in the morning,
practice centering your heart and mind on God and
begin your day by praising Him. Throughout the day,
practice praising God from your heart. If you've been
discouraged or depressed, you won't be downhearted for
long!

Chapter 6
Praise: A Reservoir of Power

I will praise thee: for thou hast heard me, and art become my salvation.

— Psalm 118:21

Christians have yet to tap into the unlimited power of praise. Praise is the greatest reservoir of power the world has yet to see demonstrated. Praise makes the power of God available to the believer. The power of God released in praise is that same power God used to make the earth and to sling the sun, moon, stars, and the universe in place. It's the same power that God used to create mankind in the beginning.

This awesome power of God can be tapped into by our sincere, heartfelt praise. We have yet to fathom the depths of power that praising God releases on our behalf. The Scriptures make it clear that one of the reasons God created man in the first place was so that man would praise God and give Him glory (Eph. 1:5,6,12). Yes, God created man to have someone to fellowship with, but He also created man to have someone to praise Him for His excellent greatness.

However, it seems that mankind doesn't always repay God with praise for all of His excellent works and the wonders He performs for them. It seems instead many people repay God with rebellion, stubbornness, and ingratitude. And every time trouble comes along, people are often quick to blame God for it. "Oh, God! Why did you allow this to happen?"

Satan is the one who robs, steals, and destroys — not God (John 10:10). God doesn't bring trouble into people's lives! That's the work of the enemy. When people accuse God of evil, they are hindering their own faith. Faith pleases God, and there is no faith in a statement that blames God for adverse circumstances. Not only does an attitude like that lack faith, it also shows much ingratitude!

Faith is what moves God. Praising God is an expression of our *faith* in Him. That's why God is moved by our praise, and that's why praise releases the power of God to work on our behalf!

God is not moved when we cry to Him in unbelief. God knows exactly where we're at and what He has promised each one of us. And He also knows His power is sufficient to see us through any test or trial.

His grace is sufficient to meet your every need if you'll learn how to praise Him in faith for what He's doing in your behalf. If you'll put your faith and trust in God and demonstrate that trust by praising Him, He will bring you through every situation to a place of victory!

So many times when circumstances look impossible, we get down in the dumps and begin to grumble and complain. But if we would praise God in the midst of the situation instead of complaining, we would put ourselves in a position where we could receive from God.

If we would just learn to let nothing but the praises of God come out of our mouth when things don't seem to be going right, we'd find the way of escape out of even

the worst situation! But so many times instead of praising God, we begin to doubt and question Him: "Why,
God? Why did You allow this to happen to me, God?"
When we do that we're really questioning God's faithfulness.

I have never read in the Bible where Jesus ever
doubted His Father's faithfulness. Nor have I ever read
in the Bible where the Apostle Paul questioned God
about the trials and tribulations he encountered, and
Paul was just as human as we are. And I don't think
any of us have suffered what Paul suffered! Paul
responded to every circumstance in faith and with
praise, and that's one reason God was able to accom-
plish so much through him.

You see, it is our duty to praise God our Creator.
Some people take exception to that, but the Word of
God has much to say about praising God. In fact, if
you'll look up the word "praise" in a concordance, you
will find that much of what the Bible has to say about
praise is found in the Book of Psalms.

PSALM 45:17
**17 I will make thy name to be remembered in all
generations: therefore shall the people praise thee
for ever and ever.**

PSALM 107:8
**8   OH THAT MEN WOULD PRAISE THE LORD
FOR HIS GOODNESS, and for his wonderful
works to the children of men!**

PSALM 117:1
**1 O praise the Lord, all ye nations: praise him, all
ye people.**

The Bible tells us that the experiences of the children of Israel are written for our admonition and as examples for us (1 Cor. 10:11). The Book of Psalms was the children of Israel's prayer and songbook. Many of the Psalms either dealt directly with praise, or indirectly with the results and benefits of praise. If the children of Israel were constantly praising God in the Psalms, how much more should we be filled with praise for our loving Heavenly Father!

The fact that there is so much about praise in the Book of Psalms should indicate to us that we need to be praising God much more than we are! We may think those of us living under the New Covenant are so advanced from the Israelites of the Old Covenant, but when it comes to praise, maybe they were ahead of us!

Men of Praise

Let's look at two Old Testament men of faith who learned the secret of praising God. For example, we can take a lesson in praise from Job, a man born under the Old Covenant, who continually praised God. People use Job as an example of a person who really had problems. But many Bible scholars believe Job's trial only lasted about nine months.

However, even in the midst of his problems, Job blessed the Lord. When it was reported to Job that his livestock, his servants, and his sons and daughters had all been killed, the Bible says that Job bowed down before God and worshipped.

JOB 1:20-22
**20 Then Job arose, and rent his mantle, and
shaved his head, and fell down upon the ground,
and worshipped,**
21 And said . . . blessed be the name of the Lord.
**22 In all this Job sinned not, nor charged God
foolishly.**

Even when Job was afflicted with boils from head to
toe, he didn't sin against God. His wife said to him,
". . . *Dost thou still retain thine integrity? curse God,
and die*" (Job 2:9). But the Bible says, ". . . *In all this
did not Job sin with his lips*" (v. 10).

Job's friends gave Job a lot of advice, but when all
was said and done, Job humbled himself before the
Lord, and God brought victory into his life. And the
Word of God declares, "*And the Lord turned the captiv-
ity of Job, when he prayed for his friends: also the Lord
gave Job twice as much as he had before*" (Job 42:10).

David Knew the Secret of Praising God!

David was another godly example of a man who
lived a life of praise. David discovered the secret of
praising God at an early age. I'm convinced that's one
reason David was able to develop such a close friend-
ship with God and why the Bible says of him, ". . . *I
have found David the son of Jesse, a man after mine
own heart, which shall fulfil all my will*" (Acts 13:22).

Nothing gets God's attention like the praises of His
people, because praise is the greatest expression of
faith and confidence in God man can render to God.

The Book of Psalms gives us some indication of the life of praise David lived, because some of these psalms were written by David. Psalm 34 is one such psalm that the Bible records as a Psalm of David, and it shows us David's heart toward God.

PSALM 34:1-3
1 I will bless the Lord at all times: his praise shall continually be in my mouth.
2 My soul shall make her boast in the Lord: the humble shall hear thereof, and be glad.
3 O magnify the Lord with me, and let us exalt his name together.

The psalmist David knew how to praise God. David sang psalms and played the harp, and David's praises pleased God and brought God's anointing on the scene many times. For example, when King Saul was troubled by an evil spirit, Saul would call upon David to sing and play for him, and Saul was comforted (1 Sam. 16:23).

If you know how to play a musical instrument, play it for the glory of God! Play it even when there isn't anyone else to hear it but God Himself!

Praise God and watch God turn your circumstances around! No matter how impossible your circumstance may seem, no matter how high those mountains in your life appear to be, no matter how impossible that dream God has planted in your heart seems to be, if you will sincerely praise God as a demonstration of your trust and confidence in Him and in His Word, God will move on your behalf.

Focus only on what God said in His Word. Keep your attention *only* on what God has promised you in His Word, because you can be sure that God will be faithful to fulfill His Word to you. And in His Word, God promised to deliver you out of *every* problem. God didn't promise to deliver you out of *half* of your problems! No, He said He would deliver you out of *all* of your problems!

> **PSALM 34:4,17,19 (*Amplified*)**
> 4   I sought (inquired of) for the Lord, and required Him [of necessity, and on the authority of His Word], and He heard me, and delivered me from ALL my fears. . . .
> 17 When the righteous cry for help, the Lord hears, and delivers them out of ALL their distress and troubles. . . .
> 19 Many evils confront the [consistently] righteous; but the Lord delivers him out of them all.

We need to get ahold of these scriptures, not just with our heads, but really meditate on them in our hearts and understand that God is willing and able to deliver us from every distressing situation.

Firmly establish in your heart that God *wants* to deliver you and that He is well *able* to deliver you, and then begin to praise Him in faith for His delivering power at work in your life.

Praising God in 'The Midnight Hour'

Notice that Paul always either begins or ends his epistles with tremendous expressions of praise or thanksgiving. Praise was a way of life to him. Many of his epistles contain the phrases, "I thank my God always," or "Blessed be God." If we follow Paul's teaching on faith, we need to follow his teaching and his example on praising God too!

Paul knew something about praising God even in the hard times. In fact, Paul is the one who said he was *". . . pressed out of measure, above strength, insomuch that we despaired even of life"* (2 Cor. 1:8). Yet Paul knew how to praise God! Look at some of the tests and trials Paul endured as he was faithful to preach the gospel.

> **2 CORINTHIANS 11:23-28**
> **23 Are they ministers of Christ? (I speak as a fool) I am more; in labours more abundant, in stripes above measure, in prisons more frequent, in deaths oft.**
> **24 Of the Jews five times received I forty stripes save one.**
> **25 Thrice was I beaten with rods, once was I stoned, thrice I suffered shipwreck, a night and a day I have been in the deep;**
> **26 In journeyings often, in perils of waters, in perils of robbers, in perils by mine own countrymen, in perils by the heathen, in perils in the city, in perils in the wilderness, in perils in the sea, in perils among false brethren;**
> **27 In weariness and painfulness, in watchings often, in hunger and thirst, in fastings often, in cold and nakedness.**
> **28 Beside those things that are without, that which cometh upon me daily, the care of all the churches.**

Did Paul complain about the trials and tribulations he endured preaching the gospel? No, Paul is the one who said, *"Rejoice in the Lord ALWAY: and again I say, Rejoice"* (Phil. 4:4).

If anyone understood praising God in the hard places it was Paul! Many were the times he could have hung his head and moaned, "Oh, Lord, poor ole me. You've got me in a mess this time, Lord. Lord, I don't know if You really knew what You were doing when You sent me *here* to preach."

For example, in Acts 16 when Paul and Silas were thrown into jail, Paul could have said, "This is one time I don't have any reason to rejoice!" And while Paul could have been bitterly complaining, his partner Silas sitting next to him in those stocks could have said, "Amen! That's right, brother! Preach it, Paul!"

ACTS 16:22-26
22 And the multitude rose up together against them: and the magistrates rent off their clothes, and commanded to beat them.
23 And when they had laid many stripes upon them, they cast them into prison, charging the jailor to keep them safely:
24 Who, having received such a charge, thrust them into the inner prison, and made their feet fast in the stocks.
25 And AT MIDNIGHT Paul and Silas prayed, and SANG PRAISES unto God: and the prisoners heard them.
26 And suddenly there was a great earthquake, so that the foundations of the prison were shaken: and immediately all the doors were opened, and every one's bands were loosed.

Even in the midnight hour when all hope seemed to be lost, and when there seemed to be no way out of the trial, Paul unwaveringly and unceasingly praised God.

Paul and Silas, their backs bleeding and their feet in stocks, were thrown into prison for preaching the gospel. In those dire circumstances, Paul and Silas learned the sacrifice of praise. After all, that prison probably wasn't the most pleasant place!

For one thing, the Bible says Paul and Silas were thrust into the *inner* prison (Acts 16:24). That means it was probably dark, cold, and uncomfortable, and there was probably no possible escape from that place!

I imagine Paul and Silas' backs were hurting from the blows they received because verse 23 says they "laid many stripes on them." And they were probably cramped and tired sitting in those stocks all night. But Paul and Silas gave God the *sacrifice* of praise. They praised God in *spite* of their circumstances, even though in the natural I'm sure they didn't feel like praising God.

Paul and Silas could have complained, griped, and grumbled instead, *and those circumstances would not have changed.* Silas could have accused Paul, saying, "Paul, why in the world did you talk me into coming on this trip with you, anyway? Look at me! Now I'm a *jailbird.*" Paul could have whined and said, "Silas, we missed God for sure this time!"

But Paul and Silas didn't murmur or complain to God. No, they sang praises to God. What a demonstration of faith! Paul and Silas sat in those stocks, their bleeding backs cut open from the whip, and the Bible says they sang praises to God.

Paul and Silas didn't praise God quietly either because the other prisoners heard them (Acts 16:25). I wouldn't be surprised if they sang at the top of their lungs, "Praise the Lord for His mercy endureth for ever. Praise the Lord, no dungeon is going to hold us down! Praise the Lord, we may be in prison now, but God is going to rescue us!"

When Paul and Silas began to sing praises to God, the very prison began to shake! As they sang praises to God that jail shook like a leaf in the wind! That kind of supernatural demonstration of faith does not come from just paying God "lip service" in mechanical, half-hearted praises to Him. That wouldn't cause a jail to shake! No, those praises were coming from their hearts!

Heartfelt praise moves God! Paul and Silas' stocks fell off and their bands were loosened! The prison doors swung open, and all the prisoners were free, including Paul and Silas. Their complete deliverance came to pass, not because they griped and complained, but because they declared God's greatness in praise!

It's also interesting that the Bible says — not tradition, not some preacher — but the *Bible* says Paul and Silas sang praises to God at midnight! I'm sure that was literally *at* midnight, yet I believe that prison experience was also a "midnight hour" in their lives.

In other words, it's never too late to sing the praises of God. No matter how bleak your situation may look and how much Satan may tempt you to think, *It's too late! God can't do anything for me now!* don't believe him. With God all things are possible (Matt. 19:26; Mark 10:27; Luke 18:27).

Believers today need to take a lesson from Paul and Silas' experience. Paul knew how to live the life of praise. Even after facing many tests and trials, Paul penned the words, *"Now thanks be unto God, which always causeth us to TRIUMPH in Christ . . . "* (2 Cor. 2:14).

The problem with many of us is that when we find ourselves in an impossible situation, instead of turning to God and magnifying *Him*, we magnify the problem! Or we look to people to help us, or at least someone who will listen to us gripe and complain: "Could you counsel me and tell me why this trial is happening to me? I'm doing what God told me to do, but look what's happened! I've given up so much for Jesus! But look at me now; I'm worse off than I ever was!"

No, our help comes from God alone.

> **PSALM 37:39,40**
> **39 But the salvation of the righteous is of the Lord: he is their strength in the time of trouble.**
> **40 And the Lord shall HELP them, and deliver them: he shall deliver them from the wicked, and save them, because they trust in him.**

But if Paul had been like most of us when he found himself in this trial, he would have had a pity party in that prison. Or he would have tried to blame someone else: "Now, Silas, you're my partner. Why in the world did you let us come down here? It's your fault we're in this mess!" And they'd have gotten into an argument right there in that prison!

You see, anyone can praise God when everything is going good. But it takes faith to praise God in the hard places. It takes faith to praise God when you're surrounded by impossibilities. It takes faith to praise God in the midst of a fiery trial.

Praising God when everything looks bleak and all hope seems lost, takes someone who *knows God* — who knows His character and His nature. Praising God in the hard times takes someone who believes God *is* who He said He *is*, and that God will *do* what He said He would *do*!

It takes faith to praise God when the storm clouds are all around you and you can't see anything but trouble. But in the midst of the storm, *act on your faith* by praising God!

For Paul and Silas, their impossibility was being cast into that prison with no way out. Praising God in the *midnight* hour when all hope of getting out of that prison was gone was their only avenue of escape! In other words, even when everything seemed hopeless, praise prevailed!

Praise releases the power of God. Through praise the power of God was released in that circumstance to set Paul and Silas free — just because they put their trust in God. Their praises demonstrated that!

When Paul and Silas surrendered themselves to God's care and praised Him, the power of God shook that jail with an earthquake: ". . . *suddenly there was a great earthquake, so that the foundations of the prison were shaken: and immediately all the doors were opened . . .*" (Acts 16:26). At the midnight hour in Paul and Silas' lives, God moved in a miraculous way in their behalf in response to their *praise!*

Your Midnight Hour

Each of us has a midnight hour at some time or another in our lives. But if we would begin to praise God even in the midst of despair or impossibilities, we would experience an "earthquake" in our circumstances too! God will "shake" those circumstances that are trying to bind us, if we'll only put our trust in Him and in His Word.

Circumstances must move out of the way just as they did for Paul and Silas. That earthquake was a demonstration of the power of God; it shook that prison and set them free! And God will give you a demonstration of His power, too, as you take Him at His Word and begin to praise His holy Name.

Another interesting aspect of this dramatic deliverance was how quickly the circumstance changed as Paul and Silas chose to praise God, instead of grumbling and complaining about their situation. It wasn't long before the same jailer who had put them in stocks was dressing their wounds and giving them something to eat!

ACTS 16:27-34
27 And the keeper of the prison awaking out of his sleep, and seeing the prison doors open, he

drew out his sword, and would have killed himself, supposing that the prisoners had been fled.
28 But Paul cried with a loud voice, saying, Do thyself no harm: for we are all here.
29 Then he called for a light, and sprang in, and came trembling, and fell down before Paul and Silas,
30 And brought them out, and said, Sirs, what must I do to be saved?
31 And they said, Believe on the Lord Jesus Christ, and thou shalt be saved, and thy house.
32 And they spake unto him the word of the Lord, and to all that were in his house.
33 And he took them the same hour of the night, and washed their stripes; and was baptized, he and all his, straightway.
34 And when he had brought them into his house, he set meat before them, and rejoiced, believing in God with all his house.

Paul and Silas' circumstances changed because they learned how to praise God instead of griping and complaining. God doesn't respond to ingratitude and complaining. God responds only to our faith which is expressed in our praises and thanksgiving to Him for what He *has* done for us and *is* doing for us, even though we may not see it yet in the natural!

Praise will bring the glorious victory when nothing else will. If you've been fasting and praying about something and you have not yet received the manifestation, start praising God!

I'm not saying to praise God *for* the trouble! God didn't bring trouble into your life in the first place! The Bible says, *"Every GOOD gift and every perfect gift is from above, and cometh down from the Father of lights . . ."* (James 1:17).

As I've said, some people have had the mistaken idea that we are to praise God *for* the evil things that happen to us in this world. But that is not in line with the overall teaching of the Bible. The Bible says to praise God *in* the midst of every circumstance, because God has promised He is going to deliver you!

Praise in the New Testament

Let's see what the New Testament has to say about praise.

1 PETER 2:9
9 But ye are a chosen generation, a royal priesthood, an holy nation, a peculiar people; THAT YE SHOULD SHEW FORTH THE PRAISES OF HIM who hath called you out of darkness into his marvellous light.

Who should show forth the praises of God? If you're a child of God, *you* should show forth God's praises because you were called out of darkness into the marvelous light of the Lord Jesus Christ. God set you free and brought you out of the miry clay and put your feet upon the solid Rock, the Lord Jesus Christ (Ps. 40:2)!

You may tremble on the Rock sometimes because of the circumstances that try to come against you in life, but the Rock will never move from underneath you. And if you will stay with the Rock, the Rock will stay with you!

MATTHEW 21:16
16 . . . Jesus saith unto them, Yea; have ye never read, Out of the mouth of babes and sucklings thou hast perfected PRAISE?

ROMANS 15:11
11 . . . PRAISE the Lord, all ye Gentiles; and LAUD him, all ye people.

EPHESIANS 1:12
12 That we should be to the PRAISE of his glory, who first trusted in Christ.

PHILIPPIANS 1:10,11
10 That ye may approve things that are excellent; that ye may be sincere and without offence till the day of Christ;
11 Being filled with the fruits of righteousness, which are by Jesus Christ, unto the glory and PRAISE of God.

HEBREWS 2:12
12 . . . I will declare thy name unto my brethren, in the midst of the church will I sing PRAISE unto thee.

REVELATION 19:5
5 . . . PRAISE our God, all ye his servants, and ye that fear him, both small and great

What Jesus Said About Praise

In the following passage, Jesus' disciples were praising Him and the Pharisees objected. The Bible says the disciples were praising God "with a loud voice." Maybe the Pharisees thought the disciples were getting carried away and overdoing it or that their praises were just an emotional outburst. But it's interesting to note that the Pharisees didn't like to hear the praises of God.

LUKE 19:37-40
**37 And when he was come nigh, even now at the
descent of the mount of Olives, the whole multitude of the disciples began to rejoice and PRAISE
God with a loud voice for all the mighty works
that they had seen;
38 Saying, Blessed be the King that cometh in the
name of the Lord: peace in heaven, and glory in
the highest.
39 And some of the Pharisees from among the
multitude said unto him, Master, rebuke thy disciples.
40 And he answered and said unto them, I tell you
that, if these should hold their peace, the stones
would immediately cry out.**

We find people in the church world today who act
like those Pharisees in Jesus' day. They don't like to
hear the praises of God. They don't like to praise God
themselves, and they don't like to hear others praising
God either!

There are congregations in the world like that today
too. They remind me of those Pharisees of old who told
Jesus to make His disciples stop praising Him. I think
we have some pharisee-type churches in the world
today. If you begin to praise God in those churches, the
ushers are likely to tell you, "Be quiet! We don't allow
that kind of emotional display in our church."

But in this passage of scripture we find out what
Jesus said about praise, because when the Pharisees
told Jesus to rebuke His disciples for praising Him,
Jesus responded, ". . . *I tell you that, if these should
hold their peace, the stones would immediately cry out*"
(Luke 19:40).

If God's creation — mankind — doesn't cry out in praise to Him for His excellent greatness, somewhere else in God's creation praises will ring out — even if the rocks have to cry out!

> **PSALM 150:1,2,6**
> **1 Praise ye the Lord. Praise God in his sanctuary: praise him in the firmament of his power.**
> **2 Praise him for his MIGHTY ACTS: praise him according to his excellent greatness. . . .**
> **6 Let every thing that hath breath praise the Lord. Praise ye the Lord.**

"Let every thing that hath breath praise the Lord . . ." (v. 6). Praise God with your mouth. Praise Him with a song! If you don't feel like singing, just lift up your voice and praise Him. Enter into God's courts with praise and receive what you need from your Heavenly Father. God desires to bless you beyond your greatest desires.

We need to learn to praise God wherever we are regardless of circumstances because the Bible says that all of God's creation is to give God praise, honor, and glory.

"Let every thing that hath breath praise the Lord. . . ." I have a big ole dog named Bear. He's part of God's creation and he breathes! It would be interesting to see how he's going to praise the Lord! Seriously though, most of you probably remember being taught in science class as a child that even plants breathe. What the Bible is saying here is that God's entire creation is to give Him praise and glory! And we're part of that creation!

Then in Romans 8:22, the Bible says that the whole creation groans for the day when it shall be removed from under the tyrannical hand of the enemy. Go back to Genesis and see the way God's universe was created in the first place. God said, "It is good" about everything He created (Gen. 1:4,10,12,18,21,25,31).

If all of God's creation is to give Him praise, how much more should we, His children praise Him! Let's be faithful to praise God, so the rocks and the trees don't have to cry out for us!

If you don't believe God can make his creation speak, read the story in the Old Testament about Balaam and his donkey (Numbers 22:21-35). Balaam was headstrong, and he was getting himself in trouble with the Lord because of it.

When Balaam went with the princes of Moab, Balaam's donkey recognized the angel of God standing in his way to prevent Balaam from going any further. The Bible says, ". . . *the angel of the Lord stood in the way for an adversary against him* [Balaam]. . . . *And the ass saw the angel of the Lord standing in the way . . .*" (Num. 22:22,23).

NUMBERS 22:27,28
27 And when the ass saw the angel of the Lord, she fell down under Balaam: and Balaam's anger was kindled, and he smote the ass with a staff.
28 And THE LORD OPENED THE MOUTH OF THE ASS, and she said unto Balaam, What have I done unto thee, that thou hast smitten me these three times?

Then the Lord opened Balaam's eyes so he could see the angel of the Lord standing in the way. But it took a donkey to get Balaam's attention! God can open the mouth of His creation if He needs to! Balaam's donkey recognized the angel of the Lord when Balaam didn't, and God spoke through one of His creatures — a donkey — to warn Balaam!

If God's man doesn't praise Him, something else in God's creation will — even if it's the rocks! Praise will come from somewhere in God's universe. God's creation needs to praise the Creator for His excellent majesty. After all, the universe and everything in it was created as an expression of God's love. Therefore, praise, thanksgiving, and gratitude should be our response to God's goodness and His greatness.

The Sacrifice of Praise

HEBREWS 13:15
15 By him therefore let us offer THE SACRIFICE OF PRAISE to God continually, that is, the fruit of our lips giving thanks to his name.

What does the Bible mean by "a sacrifice of praise"? You might say, "But I thought sacrifices were done away with under the Old Covenant!"

Yes, the sacrificial system of offering the blood of animals as an atonement for sin was done away with when Jesus ushered in the New Covenant with His own blood. Therefore, we no longer sacrifice the blood of bulls or goats as an atonement for sin. Jesus Christ did that once and for all in the sacrifice of Himself (Heb. 9:12-28).

However, under the New Covenant an acceptable sacrifice to God is the *sacrifice of praise*. That means praising God when we don't necessarily feel like praising Him.

Then under the New Covenant we are also to present our bodies as a living sacrifice. God honors these sacrifices (Rom. 12:1). The Bible calls this our reasonable service.

But there's something we need to understand in order to more fully comprehend what the Bible means by "a sacrifice of praise." The natural man — this physical man on the outside — contacts the natural world with the five senses. The spirit man on the inside contacts the spirit world through the spirit.

If you have been born again, your spirit is in contact with God. But even if you have been born again, the natural man on the outside — your body — has not been born again.

What significance does this have to praising God? It has a lot to do with praising God because even if you are born again, your body is still fleshly or carnal and it doesn't necessarily want to praise God. But your spirit is to have dominion or control over your body; your spirit is to be in authority.

Your body is just the house you live in. The real you is the spirit man on the inside. The spirit man — the real *you* — dwells inside of your body which is the natural house you live in (2 Peter 1:13,14; 2 Cor. 5:1,4).

Romans 8:7 says the carnal mind and nature ". . . *is enmity against God: for it is not subject to the law of God, neither indeed can be.*" Your body and fleshly nature is at enmity with God; your body and your mind are not subject to the law of God because they are not born again. That's why your mind has to be renewed by the Word of God and your body has to be kept under the subjection of your spirit (Rom. 12:1,2; 1 Cor. 9:27).

That's what Paul meant when he said, ". . . *I keep under my body . . .*" (1 Cor. 9:27), or in other words, "I keep my body under subjection to my spirit and tell my body what to do!"

The real "you" — the man on the inside — must tell your body what it's going to do! That's why sometimes *you* have to make your body cooperate in praising God even when it doesn't *feel* like it.

Many Christians have not understood that their body or their flesh is not born again, so they've felt condemned when they didn't *feel* like praising God. But many times the man on the outside won't feel like praising God, but your spirit man always wants to praise God.

If you understand this, you won't feel condemned when you don't feel like praising God. Just realize that the real *you* is the man on the inside (1 Thess. 5:23; 1 Peter 3:3,4; 2 Cor. 4:16), and your spirit always wants to praise God.

That spirit man on the inside is the one who is to be in control and dominate the outward man, your body. The spirit man on the inside is to bring your body into subjection. Your spirit man on the *inside* is the one who is to dominate the flesh or your carnal nature — the man on the *outside*.

The devil can contact your mind because the Word of God says the devil is the god of this natural world (2 Cor. 4:4). Therefore, the enemy can contact you in the natural in your mind and through your flesh because that's the realm he influences.

For example, when the devil tries to attack you in the area of doubt, instead of siding in with him and your carnal mind, let your spirit dominate you. If you've been diligent to feed your spirit on the Word of God, the Word will come up out of your spirit and defeat the enemy in every battle.

The devil will try to tell you every lie and will always try to make you feel condemned. And if you agree with him and believe his lies, you will fall into condemnation. That's how he tries to keep the believer defeated and unsuccessful in life.

If you have sinned but you've already confessed your sin to God, and the enemy tries to bring guilt and condemnation against you, put him in his place with the Word of God. Don't receive the condemnation of the enemy. The Bible says, *"If we confess our sins, he is faithful and just to forgive us our sins, and to cleanse us from all unrighteousness"* (1 John 1:9).

Therefore, if you've confessed your sin to God, He has forgiven you. So when Satan tries to come against you with condemnation, begin to enter into praise and worship because he can't stand it when God's people magnify their Heavenly Father!

The enemy has used this area of condemnation to wreak havoc in the lives of many Christians. But if you're born again, you have authority over the devil (Matt. 18:18; Luke 10:19). Jesus has already defeated Satan, and you have victory over him because ". . . *greater is he that is in you, than he that is in the world*" (1 John 4:4). If you're born again, the Greater One is on the inside of you.

Therefore, when the devil tries to come to you with his lies, let the man on the inside rise up big within you. The Bible says Satan is the father of lies (John 8:44), so he can't speak the truth. Therefore, don't listen to him — he's a liar!

No matter what lies the devil tries to tell you, you've got the Greater One on the inside of you who will lead and guide you into all truth and dispel those lies (John 16:13). Satan is a defeated foe, and the Greater One on the inside of you can put you over in life.

Learn how to let the Holy Spirit on the inside of you dominate. Let the Spirit of God flow from within you, use the Word of God, and put the devil on the run. Tell the devil, "I rebuke you, devil. I resist you in the Name of Jesus, and you've got to flee from me. Praise the Lord!" Then begin to shout and praise the Lord.

Don't Be Led by Feelings

"But I don't *feel* like praising the Lord. I'm too tired. I don't *feel* like shouting." That's all right. Just begin to declare the praises of God anyway, and soon you'll *feel* like shouting! You won't be able to contain the praises of God. They'll just flow from you in victory!

There are many things in life we don't always *feel* like doing. For example, do you always *feel* like getting out of bed in the morning and going to work? No! Some days you don't especially *feel* like going to work, but you do it anyway. That's where discipline comes in! No matter how much your body wants to stay in bed, you get up and go to work anyway.

If you can discipline yourself in one area of life, you can discipline yourself in other areas too. So discipline yourself to rejoice in the Lord and praise Him. Learn to cultivate a life of praise and worship to God. Learn to take authority over the enemy when you need to, and do not let him have his way in your life. You have authority over Satan through your position in Christ, and your praises to God put the enemy to flight!

Actually, the further away you live from God and His Word, the louder the clamour and the lies of the devil will be. The closer you live to God in praise and in His Word, the stronger spiritually you will become, and the easier it will be for you to discern the lies of the enemy and to stand against them.

The more you praise God, the less effective Satan's deceptions are to you because the enemy will not stay in your presence for long if you are praising the Lord. I don't mean to imply that the devil will completely leave you alone, because he won't — at least not while you're on this earth. The Bible doesn't teach that.

Satan will always try to get you depressed and keep you defeated. He'll try to tell you the same lies over and over again. He'll subtly whisper in your ear that you're a failure and that your life will never amount to anything.

Particularly if Satan has ever succeeded in getting you trapped into thinking of yourself as a failure and always defeated in life, he'll try to come back to get you to keep on thinking that same way. That's what the Bible means by "the wiles" of the devil. But we are not ignorant of his devices (2 Cor. 2:11; Eph. 6:11).

Satan doesn't change his tactics, especially if he finds he's been successful in one area of your life. He'll keep trying to wear you down with his tactics, and he'll continually try to bring you into bondage with his lies. But if you'll resist him, he *will* flee (James 4:7).

You see, the Bible says Satan is already a defeated foe. Jesus whipped him at the Cross. Therefore, you can overcome him in every one of his schemes against you, and one way you do that is by using the Word against him and praising God. The devil doesn't like the praises of God. Shut the door on him by praising and thanking your Heavenly Father for delivering you.

Don't Look at Circumstances — Look to the Word!

Carnal Christians are Christians who walk by sight, not by faith. They don't usually enjoy the life of praise because they usually look at the circumstances to determine victory — not at God and at His Word. Therefore, they wouldn't be accustomed to praising God based just on their faith in God's Word; they would be more inclined to praise God once the circumstances began to *look* good.

And carnal Christians would probably get embarrassed when other people praise God in their presence, because praising God is usually not a habit with them.

It's interesting that Paul called the Corinthians carnal even though they had every gift of the Spirit operating in their lives! Just because people have gifts of the Spirit operating in their lives or in their church is no sign they're spiritual or their church is spiritual.

Also, people who are bound by fear, timidity, doubt, and unbelief are usually not walking consistently in praise. One of the best ways to overcome fear, is to begin to magnify and exalt God and meditate on how great *He* is. No matter how big your fear is, it will flee in the light of *God's* greatness.

Is it possible to be too extravagant, or too lavish in praising God? No! Let us offer the *sacrifice* of praise to God continually. Praise is to be the fruit of our lips.

> **HEBREWS 13:15**
> **15 By Him therefore let us offer the sacrifice of praise to God continually, that is, the fruit of our lips giving thanks to his name.**

Psalm 34:1 said, "*I will bless the Lord at all times: his praise shall continually be in my mouth.*" Praising God for who He *is* — is the very heart and core of worship.

Praise is the true gate by which we are to enter into a dimension of the Presence of God that the Church has yet to experience. Oh, we've experienced a little of the Presence of God. But if we would enter into God's Presence through the gate of praise as the Bible tells us to, we would find that we can come into a place of praise and worship that the Church of the Lord Jesus Christ has yet to experience.

If you want to find yourself in total victory, first make sure you are obedient to God and His Word in every area. Make sure you're living a life of consecration to God in every area of your life. Then learn to consistently praise God from a heart of love and appreciation.

Only those of us who have been born again can truly understand praise. The Bible says, *"The dead praise not the Lord, neither any that go down into silence"* (Ps. 115:17).

You say, "Of course, the dead can't praise the Lord!" But I don't believe the Bible is just talking about those who have ceased to live in mortal bodies. I think this verse is also referring to those who have never experienced the quickening power of the Spirit of God in the new birth. I believe this scripture also refers to spiritually dead people. People who are spiritually dead have no inclination or desire to praise God.

Only those who have been born again and understand the grace and power and faithfulness of God have the right to appropriate the blessings of praise in their lives. Christians truly are privileged to be able to praise the Creator of their very existence.

Victory is always assured when you stand in faith on God's Word. And when you praise God before you actually see your victory, that's a *sacrifice* of praise. God recognizes the *sacrifice of praise*. He will intervene in your affairs to give you the desires of your heart as you learn the sacrifice of praise — praising Him before you *see* your circumstances change.

I believe every Christian would experience a fuller, richer, more dynamic life if each one of us would only consistently praise God. Sometimes it takes will power to begin to praise God. I'm not talking about praising God just when we feel good, or when we've been especially uplifted in a church service.

We can always praise the Lord because His mercy endures forever! Even if you're going through a trial and you're feeling forsaken and if this one scripture is all you can hang on to, I challenge you to stand in faith on that scripture and watch God move in your behalf!

God responds to praise. If you don't feel like praising God because you think He has forsaken you, the Word declares that God will never leave you nor forsake you (Heb. 13:5). Just begin to encourage your own heart by saying, "Praise the Lord for His mercy endures forever!"

If you want a life full of joy, if you want to learn how to walk deeper in God and receive the desires of your heart, if you want to be set free from whatever may have you bound, begin to enter into the praises of God as a lifestyle. Don't just keep asking Him for the same petition over and over again! If your request is in line with God's Word, simply begin to praise Him because He has promised to answer you!

To put it simply, you play a major part in whether you get out of the depression or despair or the test or trial that would try to keep you down. It is up to you because there *is* a way of escape! God's Word promises us a way of escape out of any difficulty.

So if you're tempted to doubt God or His faithfulness to His Word, or to give way to despair, if you'll begin to praise God out of a sincere heart, you will find that you have tapped into a power source that will take you far beyond your own strengths and abilities.

Standing on God's Word in absolute faith and confidence and praising God for your victory before you see it manifest in the natural will take you beyond the natural. It will take you beyond what you have ever imagined or could ever think possible, because God's ways and His power are so far and high above our ways or ability. It's impossible for us to imagine His unfathomable love (Eph. 3:20; Isa. 55:8,9).

God promised in Ephesians 3:20, *"Now unto him that is able to do exceeding abundantly above all that we ask or think, according to the power that worketh in us."* Don't trust in your own might or strength because the Word says it's *". . . Not by might, nor by power, but by my spirit, saith the Lord of hosts"* (Zech. 4:6). God responds to our praise.

If you need healing, reach out by your faith and appropriate God's Word and receive your healing. Then begin to thank and praise God because He is faithful to His Word and He has heard and answered your petition. If you need deliverance from a habit or anything that has held you in bondage, it is available in God. Ask God to set you free, and then praise Him for your deliverance!

Practice speaking forth the praises of God. Cursing God is a way of life for many of the unsaved. Praising God should be the lifestyle of God's children. Let praise become a way of life for you, not just something you do once in a while. Let praising God become so natural to you that you just automatically praise God.

Make this your prayer:

Father, I pray that You would help me establish a new lifestyle — a lifestyle of praise and worship unto You. Thank You, Father, because I know You have heard and answered all of my petitions. Now by faith I'm going to praise You for every answer. Father, it is my earnest desire to let Your praises continually flow from my lips. In Jesus' Name, amen.